HAMP
THE NE

WALKS FOR MOTORISTS

Roberta MacLaren

★

30 Walks with sketch maps

COUNTRYSIDE BOOKS
NEWBURY, BERKSHIRE

*Countryside Books' walking guides cover most areas of England
and include the following series:*

*County Rambles
Walks For Motorists
Exploring Long Distance Paths
Literary Walks
Pub Walks*

A complete list is available from the publisher.

Originally Published
by Frederick Warne Ltd

This edition published 1993

© Roberta MacLaren 1993

COUNTRYSIDE BOOKS
3 Catherine Road
Newbury, Berkshire

ISBN 1 85306 215 4

Cover photograph taken near Kingsclere
by Andy Williams

Publisher's Note

At the time of publication all footpaths used in these walks were
designated as official footpaths or rights of way, but it should be borne in
mind that diversion orders may be made from time to time.
Although every care has been taken in the preparation of this Guide,
neither the Author nor the Publisher can accept responsibility for those
who stray from the Rights of Way.

Produced through MRM Associates Ltd., Reading
Typeset by Wessex Press Design & Print Limited, Warminster
Printed in England by J. W. Arrowsmith Ltd., Bristol

Contents

Introduction

Situated in the centre of England's south coast, Hampshire is bordered by Dorset and Wiltshire to the west, Berkshire to the north and Surrey and West Sussex in the east. It is a county of sharp contrasts, its landscape including wide expanses of open heathland, dense woodland and softly rolling hills.

In the east, where the western extremity of the Weald stretches over the county border, the scenery is very reminiscent of that to be found in Surrey and West Sussex. Here there are high hills, many of which are called hangers, and areas of delightful woodland.

In the north-west are the Hampshire Downs; a range of high chalk hills stretching north into Berkshire. Their steep slopes and open hilltops afford magnificent views that make walking in the area well worthwhile. Some of the downs are used for sheep farming or the growing of cereal crops but the training of racehorses is also a thriving industry here.

Another belt of chalk downland runs across the middle of the county but in the south-west the scenery changes abruptly. Most of this area is covered by the New Forest, William of Normandy's finest legacy to the nation that he conquered and Hampshire's most popular tourist attraction. Although it is called a forest, much of the area is open heathland and is particularly beautiful during the summer months when the heather is in bloom.

Because the forest was originally used for hunting, the local peasants were forbidden to erect fences and their domestic animals were allowed to roam freely. This practice gave rise to the commoners' rights that are in force today; cattle, pigs, sheep and donkeys still run free in the forest and mingle with the famous New Forest ponies which are also owned by the local residents.

Besides its wealth of varied scenery Hampshire also possesses a long and interesting history. Because of its position it was long ago subject to invasions by nomadic tribes from the continent. Some left little trace of their passing whilst others built durable structures such as Grim's Ditch and the hill fort on Danebury Hill. During the Roman period the town of Calleva was built in the northern part of the county and the Saxons made Winchester the capital of England.

Thus Hampshire has something to interest everybody, whether they are keen on history, nature study or simply enjoying the splendours of the countryside. However, before setting out to explore, there are a few things that must be remembered.

Firstly, parts of the county can be rather muddy. Every care has been taken in planning these walks to avoid the most boggy places but it is always best to wear waterproof footwear.

Secondly, although dogs are allowed on the majority of these walks, they must be kept under proper control. This is particularly important in areas where sheep or game birds are kept.

Every walk in the book is accompanied by a simple sketch map designed to give the walker an idea of the route to be taken but they are not drawn to scale. For those who desire a more detailed map the number of the OS Landranger Series Sheet covering the area is given at the beginning of each walk.

Roberta MacLaren
Spring 1993

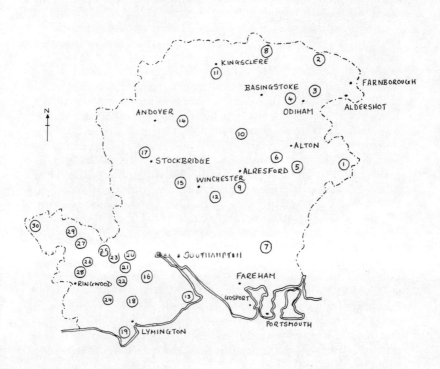

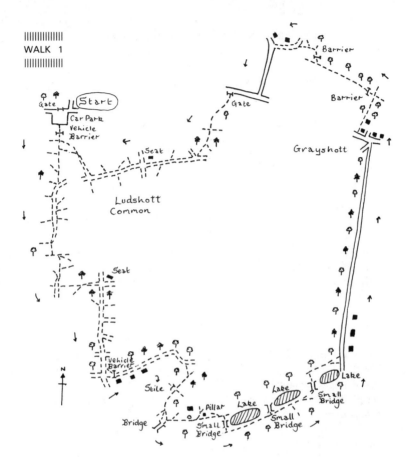

WAGGONERS WELLS

WALK 1

★

4½ miles (7 km)

OS Landranger 186

Set right on the Hampshire-Surrey border, Waggoners Wells is one of the most delightful places in the county. Magnificent beech woods surround the chain of lakes that give it its name and it is home to a wide variety of birds including heron. The woodland was purchased for the nation in 1919 as a memorial to Sir Robert Hunter who had always taken a keen interest in the preservation of public open spaces.

From Ludshott Common there are beautiful views across the wooded valleys that are so very reminiscent of the area around the Devil's Punch Bowl in neighbouring Surrey. The common itself is a wide expanse of open heathland which forms a natural habitat for many species of flora and fauna.

Parts of this walk can be rather muddy and waterproof footwear is advisable especially after rain.

Take the B3002 from Bordon travelling towards Hindhead. Follow it through Headley Down and, just after the houses on the right end, park in the first National Trust car park on Ludshott Common. This is on the right just opposite a field gate and a lane on the left.

Start the walk by going through a gap in the vehicle barrier at the rear of the car park and following the path straight ahead. This is almost immediately crossed by another path but ignore it and carry straight on, disregarding a path to the left and two others leading to houses behind the trees on the right.

Not far beyond these the path joins a track which comes from the left at a point where yet another small path goes towards the houses on the right. Follow the track straight ahead ignoring a path to the right and then another two to the left. Where the track is crossed by another path still carry straight on. The track goes down a slope and divides into two paths. Keep to the left-hand one which leads straight ahead down a steep bank.

At the bottom the path meets another in a T-junction. Turn left and, where it forks three ways, take the right-hand branch. This

7

leads up a slope at the top of which it is joined by another path from the left. Ignore this and go straight on to where, having been joined by a path from the right and swung left slightly to widen into a broad track, it is crossed by another path. Turn left on to this and follow it through the trees, ignoring a grassy path which converges with it from the right.

The path slowly widens into a track which is crossed by another at a point where there is a seat on the left. Turn right and follow the track through the wood, ignoring a path that crosses it in the valley and two turnings to the left at the top of the next slope. Not far beyond this the track is crossed by another. Carry straight on, passing some fire beaters on your right, until you come to a second cross track. This is marked 'Bridleway'.

Turn left here and follow the track past a bungalow on the right. Beyond this the track goes straight ahead for some distance before swinging to the right. Then it soon swings left again and at this point a path marked 'Bridleway' leads down a slope to the right. Turn on to this and, where it divides, follow the branch round to the right keeping the fence on your right.

The path can become rather muddy as it descends the slope but, if this is the case, it is possible to walk along the bank beside it. Ignore a stile in the fence on the right at a point where a path comes down the slope on the left and continue along the main path. Where this divides, keep to the left-hand branch and follow it to where it swings right to cross a bridge over a stream.

Leave the path just before the bridge to take another, narrower, path to the left. Disregard a path leading up to a house on the left and go straight on to pass the wishing well on your left. Beyond this the path divides. Take the right-hand branch, passing a National Trust collection pillar on your left.

The path continues to follow the bank of the stream on the right. It is joined by another path from the left and then divides at the edge of a lake. Turn right over a low bridge and follow the path to the far side of the lake where it joins another in a T-junction. Turn left on to this path.

Beyond the head of the lake the path follows a stream on the left for a short distance to reach another expanse of water. Disregard a path that crosses a small bridge on the left and carry straight on along the side of the second lake, ignoring a path which leads away through a valley to the right.

Where the path divides keep to the left-hand branch and, at the beginning of the third lake, turn left to cross another small bridge over the stream. This will take you to the far side of the lake. Turn right on to a path bordering the water and where the path divides choose either branch. Both emerge on to a lane.

Follow this lane to the left. It climbs steadily up a gentle slope and eventually joins the road. Cross over and turn left again. This will take you across a small side road called Waggoners Way just beyond which a path signposted 'Footpath' leads away to the right. Follow this to where it is crossed by another at the top of a steep slope and then turn left.

The path goes through a barrier and then skirts the edge of a wood on the right for some distance before being joined by a second path which comes through another barrier on the right. Turn right on to this and just beyond the barrier turn sharp left, ignoring a signposted footpath which leads straight ahead.

Where the path divides keep to the left-hand branch, which will bring you to a track that curves round to the right. Do not follow it to the right. Carry straight on and when you reach a lane turn left. This will bring you to where the lane joins the road. Turn right to walk along the verge for about 100 yards and then cross over to take a path labelled 'Bridleway' which runs between wooden fences.

There is a cross path where the fence on the right ends but ignore it and carry straight on for a short distance to where the path divides. Take the right-hand fork. It goes through the trees to join a track. Turn right on to this, ignoring a narrower track which diverges from it to the right, and follow it up a slight slope.

Ignore a narrow path to the right and a wider one to the left and, where the track is crossed by another track at a point where there is a seat on the right, still carry straight on. Disregard two more paths to the right, one to the left and then another to the right and you will eventually come to a place where there is a track to the right and a path to the left. Turn right on to the track and follow it to where, having ignored a path which diverges from it to the left, the main path narrows and is crossed by another. Turn right again here to return to the car park.

EVERSLEY

WALK 2

4 miles (6 km)

OS Landranger 186

The small village of Eversley was the home of Charles Kingsley, author of *The Water Babies*. He was rector here from 1842 until his death in 1875 and his body lies in the churchyard of the church that he served.

To the west of Eversley lies Warren Heath, a densely wooded area owned by the Forestry Commission. It was once part of the land belonging to Bramshill House.

Take the A33 from Basingstoke travelling towards Reading and after 8 miles turn right opposite the Wellington Memorial on to a road signposted 'Heckfield 1 — Bramshill 2 — Eversley 4'. Go straight ahead at the roundabout and where the road swings right take the side road leading straight ahead and signposted 'Bramshill Police College (Heavy Vehicles)'. Follow this for about 3 miles to where some overhead electricity cables cross the road to pass under another line on the right. Turn left here into the car park marked 'Bramshill Forest, Bramshill Common Wood'.

Cross the road and follow the metalled track straight ahead through the vehicle barrier. Having passed under the power lines turn left on to a footpath that runs parallel to the track for a short distance, skirting the pine trees on the left. Sometimes in the height of summer the first few yards of this path can become overgrown. If this is the case, keep to the track for a short distance to where an alternative entrance to the path skirts a Forestry Commission sign on the left.

After a short distance the path curves to the left into the trees at a point where it is joined by another short path from the track on the right. Follow the path through the trees to a point where three paths meet and then turn right. The path leads down into a dip, where it is crossed by a narrower path, and then on up the next slope to a barrier. Beyond this it veers to the right and widens into a track. Ignore a narrow path and a track to the left and carry straight on to reach a clearing.

Turn left and cross the clearing, passing one track on the left to reach a second one. This leads down a slight slope and then up again to a place where five tracks meet. Take the one straight ahead marked 'Private — Footpath to church only'.

Where the track swings right, follow the path straight ahead, passing a 'Private Property' sign on your right. The path runs along the edge of a private wood to reach a field gate. Pass through the gap beside it to cross the stile straight ahead and then follow the edge of the field to a gate in the far corner.

Do not go through the gate. Turn left beside it to cross another stile and then follow the fence on the right to a third stile that gives access to a plank bridge. Beyond this carry straight on, keeping the hedge on your right and ignoring a field entrance on the right to reach the wood at the far side of the field. Here a stile marks the beginning of a path that skirts a ditch on the right. It leads through the trees and crosses a small bridge to reach a metal

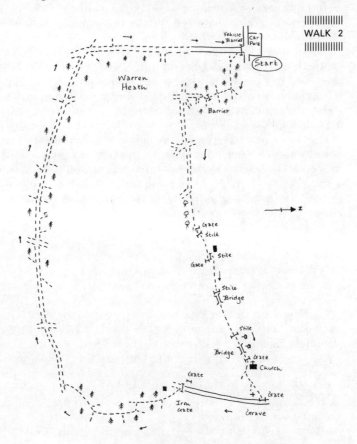

WALK 2

11

gate opening on to the churchyard.

Turn right to pass the church on your left and follow the path round the church, ignoring a branch to the right opposite the porch. Just as the ornamental trees begin to line the path, a narrow turning to the right leads to Charles Kingsley's grave.

Carry on along the main path to the churchyard gate and turn right to follow the lane. Go through the iron gate at the end and immediately left on to a footpath that passes a bungalow on the right. Ignore a turning to the left and carry on up the slope to where the path divides. Take the left-hand fork which is joined almost immediately by a path from the left and then swings right. Within a short distance it is joined by another path from the left. Ignore this and keep to the main path.

Where the path divides to skirt an area of younger trees, turn right. This will lead you across the end of another path on the right and then left to cut between the mature trees on the right and the young ones on the left. Where the younger trees end, the path crosses a ditch and joins a track.

Turn right and follow the track, ignoring another track that crosses it, a path to the right and then another to the left. This will bring you to a place where there is a second cross track. Carry on for a short distance beyond it, disregarding another path to the right, and, where the track swings right, leave it to take another leading straight ahead.

Keep to this track ignoring all side turnings until it forks at a place where a path joins it from the left. Take the left-hand branch of the track. This leads straight ahead and eventually joins a gravel track. Turn right and follow the gravel track to where it joins the head of a lane that leads down to the road and the car park.

THE BASINGSTOKE CANAL

WALK 3

★

3 miles (4.5 km)

OS Landranger 186

The Basingstoke Canal was built during the latter half of the 18th century when canal boats were one of the most popular means of transporting merchandise, but it never proved to be a very successful project. This was due partly to the fact that it did not connect up with any of the country's more important canals and partly to the fierce competition provided by road and sea transport.

The canal limped its way through the first two decades of the 19th century as a marginally profitable concern but its fate was sealed by the railway from London which was built in the 1830s. It gained a short respite in the years immediately after 1854 when large quantities of building materials were shipped along it for the construction of Aldershot Camp, but by the end of the century all traffic on it had ceased. A last attempt to reopen it was made during the First World War when the army took control of the eastern end to shift government stores and munitions, but that was of short duration. It lay deserted until the Surrey and Hampshire Canal Society was formed in 1966. Due to their persuasion Surrey and Hampshire County Councils purchased the canal in 1974 and since then a great amount of restoration work has been done upon it. Much of this work can be seen on the very attractive stretch of waterway which runs through Winchfield and Dogmersfield. Here the canal has been dredged, the tow-path cleared and bridges rebuilt.

There are a particularly large number of bridges in this area; a fact bearing witness to the canal builders' obligation to make concessions to local needs. Some of these bridges, such as Sprats Hatch Bridge, were built to serve hamlets. Others, such as Stacey Bridge, were built to connect farmland and were named after the local farmers of the time.

The canal makes a large loop to the north to avoid a park that was once the property of Sir Henry St John. In this park lies Tundry Pond, across which the canal builders were asked to build a bridge, completely unconnected with their work on the canal, to

13

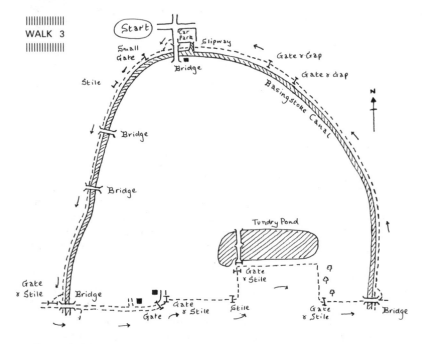

allow carriages to reach Dogmersfield House. A small village once stood on the banks of the pond but this was removed by the landowner when the park was landscaped.

On the banks of the canal to the east of Tundry Pond are some old wartime defences. These consist of pill boxes and heavy brick and concrete blocks which were hastily erected in July 1940 when invasion seemed imminent.

Take the A323 from Hartley Wintney travelling towards Fleet. Follow it for 1½ miles and, having passed under the bridge carrying the motorway, turn right on to the road marked 'Winchfield 1 — Dogmersfield 2'. This road passes Winchfield Court on the left to reach a crossroads with the Barley Mow public house on the right. Go straight across on to the no through road and park in the car park on the left. This is marked 'Barley Mow car park and slipway'.

Start the walk by going back through the car park entrance and turning left to follow the lane for a short distance. Just before the bridge turn right on to a narrow path which leads down to the tow-path and then follow the tow-path to the right.

Within a short distance the path passes through a small gate with a gap beside it and then leads on to where there is a stile on

14

the right. Ignore this and carry on along the canal bank, passing under Stacey Bridge and Baseley Bridge to Sprats Hatch Bridge.

Just before Sprats Hatch Bridge bear right on to a narrow path that leads up the bank to a gate and stile beside the bridge. Climb the stile and turn left to cross the bridge. Ignore a footpath to the right on the far side and follow the track straight ahead. This will lead you to a gate that opens on to the head of a lane. Turn right at this point to cross a stile beside a field gate and walk straight ahead to leave the field by a stile on the far side.

Turn left to skirt the next field, keeping the fence on your left. This will bring you to a gate and stile in the corner of the field that gives access to the grass bordering Tundry Pond. Turn right and follow the bank of the pond. At this point there are good views of Dogmersfield House which stands on the far side of some fields to the right.

At the far end of the grassy area bordering the pond, turn right and walk to the far corner of the wood. Here there is another gate and stile. Turn left to cross the stile and follow the track to the bridge.

Go over the bridge and turn sharp left to take a path leading down to the canal bank, then turn right to follow the tow-path. It is here that the old wartime fortifications can be seen on the far side of the canal.

After some distance the tow-path passes through two gates, each with a gap beside it, and then continues to where the Barley Mow slipway leads down to the water just before Barley Mow Bridge. Turn right at this point into the car park.

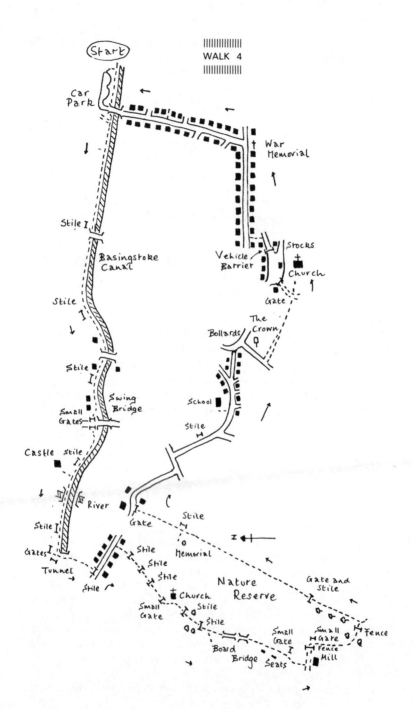

Start

||||||||||||||
WALK 4
||||||||||||||

Car Park

War Memorial

Stile I

Basingstoke Canal

Vehicle Barrier

Stocks

Church

Stile

Gate

The Crown

Bollards

Stile

Swing Bridge

School

Small Gates

Stile

Castle

Stile

River

Stile

Gate

Stile

Gates

Memorial

Tunnel

Stile

Stile

Stile

Stile

Nature Reserve

Gate and Stile

Church

Small Gate

Stile

Stile

Small Gate

Small Gate

Fence

Board Bridge

Seats

Fence

Mill

ODIHAM
AND GREYWELL

WALK 4

★

5½ miles (8.5 km)

OS Landranger 186

Odiham is one of the most interesting and picturesque of the small Hampshire towns. Many of the houses in the wide main street date from the 18th and early 19th centuries and the church is the biggest in the northern part of Hampshire. Its tower was built during the Civil War and beside the churchyard wall the stocks and whipping post are to be seen.

To the north of Odiham the Basingstoke Canal winds its way towards North Warnborough and Greywell. This is one of the most interesting stretches of the canal and one that has recently undergone a great deal of restoration. Just west of North Warnborough is a swing bridge that is still fully functional and can be raised in only one and a half minutes.

Beside the canal between North Warnborough and Greywell stand the remains of King John's Castle. This was built during the first decade of the 13th century at the order of King John who used it as a hunting lodge and a place at which to break his journeys between Windsor and Winchester. It was from this castle that the king rode to Runnymede in 1215 to set his seal on the Magna Carta. During the following year the castle was besieged by Louis, Dauphin of France, and in the 14th century it was the prison of King David of Scotland.

Once King John's Castle was an impressive place but now little remains except the ruins of the octagonal keep. Parts of the outer bailey were destroyed during the 18th century when the canal was cut through it and the surrounding moat.

Greywell church is possibly one of the churches in this part of Hampshire that are mentioned in the Domesday Book. It is very old and has several interesting features including a roodloft.

Greywell Mill, set on a particularly beautiful stretch of the river Whitewater, was functional until 1933. The enormous elmwood water wheel is still to be seen beneath a roof at the end of the building.

The Wallace Memorial Reserve is an area of marshland owned

17

by the Hampshire Wildlife Trust. It was named after E. C. Wallace, an eminent botanist, and is the habitat of several species of rare plants and insects.

Leave the M3 at junction 5 and turn on to the A287, signposted Farnham, then follow the signs to Odiham. On the outskirts of the town the road swings left at a point where the A32 to Alton goes straight ahead. Ignore the Alton road and continue along the main street until you come to the war memorial on the right. Turn left here on to a road signposted 'The Vine Church — Basingstoke Canal — Water Witch PH'. Follow this road to its end and then turn right into Odiham Wharf car park.

Start the walk by taking the narrow path at the far end of the car park and then turn right to follow the tow-path. Disregard the path that leads up to the road at the far end of Odiham Wharf and carry on under Colt Hill Bridge, ignoring a track to the right on the far side. Continue along the tow-path passing a bridge that gives access to fields on the far side of the canal and two stiles on the right. Go under another bridge and keep to the tow-path, ignoring a third stile on the right. After some distance the tow-path passes through a small gate with a gap beside it and joins the lane that crosses the swing bridge. Go straight over this to take the next section of the tow-path. It leads through another small gate, passes a stile on the right and is joined by a path that gives access to the remains of King John's Castle on the right.

Beyond the path to the castle the tow-path passes the place where the river Whitewater flows beneath the canal. This was originally achieved by channelling the river water through wooden pipes laid under the bed of the canal and it worked very well. When these pipes were replaced in 1975 they were still in a good state of preservation in spite of having been in use for 200 years.

Ignoring another stile to the right, continue along the tow-path to the mouth of the Greywell Tunnel. Follow the path up the slope beside the tunnel mouth and, disregarding a footpath to the right, turn left to pass across the top of it. From here a narrow path leads between gardens to the road.

Cross the stile at the end of this path and turn left to follow the road through Greywell village. Just beyond Chapel Lodge on the right, turn right on to a footpath that runs between fences to a stile. Beyond this go straight ahead, crossing two more stiles to reach the church at the far side of the meadows.

Go through the small gate into the churchyard and bear right beside the porch to take a narrow path that skirts the tower and crosses the churchyard to reach a stile. Beyond this the path passes between some bushes to another stile and then leads on across the water meadows. Ignore a narrow path to the right and carry straight on along a board walk that ends in a narrow bridge. This gives access to the river bank. Walk on along it until you come to a small gate and then bear right beside it to follow the fence on the right.

This will bring you to Greywell Mill. Turn left to follow the track along the front of it and then sharp right beside the remains of the water wheel, to be seen beneath a roof at the far end of the building, on to a footpath that passes through a gap in a fence.

Ignore a small gate to the left and follow the path along the water's edge to where it veers to the left through the bushes. It passes through another gap in a fence and then divides. Take the left-hand fork which is labelled 'Bridleway'. It passes between a hedge on the right and a wood on the left to reach a gate with a stile beside it. This is the entrance to the Wallace Memorial Reserve.

Follow the fence on the right. This will lead you across the upper part of the nature reserve with the marshes on your left. Ignore a stile set in the fence on the right at a point where a path leads down to a memorial stone on the left, and carry straight on to reach a gate that opens on to the road. Turn right to follow the road up the hill and at the T-junction turn left and then right again on to a road marked 'Odiham ¾ — South Warnborough 2½'.

Disregard a stile in the fence to the left and follow the road round to the left. This will lead you past the secondary school on your left. Not far beyond this the road swings sharp left again. Cross over at this point and take the 'no through road' marked West Street. This will lead you through some bollards to the main road.

Turn right on to the road to Alton and, having passed a public house called The Crown on your left, turn left into a narrow lane labelled 'Footpath'. The lane quickly narrows to a path that leads to the edge of the churchyard. Here it crosses a drive. Turn left to follow the drive down to the churchyard gate and then right to pass the stocks and whipping post on your right.

At the far side of the square bear slightly left to pass between 'Little Court' and 'The Bury Cottage' on to a lane obstructed by a vehicle barrier. Pass one more cottage on the left beyond the barrier and turn left into an alley that leads to the main street. Cross the road and turn right. This will bring you to the road on the left signposted 'Vine Church — Basingstoke Canal — Water Witch PH'. Turn left to follow it back to the canal and the car park.

SELBORNE

WALK 5

★

3 miles (4.5 km)

OS Landranger 186

The attractive little village of Selborne, nestling beneath its high tree-clad hanger, was once the home of the famous naturalist Gilbert White. It is set in one of the most beautiful parts of Hampshire; a place abounding with a wide variety of wildlife, including many rare species.

Gilbert White was born in the village in 1720 and lived in The Wakes, the family home, from 1729 until his death in 1793. He was a curate but his consuming interest always lay in the natural history of the area in which he lived. It was at The Wakes that he wrote *The Natural History and Antiquities of Selborne* — a book that served to make both the author and his village famous. Today The Wakes is a museum owned by The Oates Memorial Trust. Its lower rooms are devoted to information relating to the naturalist, whilst on the upper floor are items connected with the life of Captain Oates who died with Scott on his ill-fated expedition to the South Pole in 1912.

Gilbert White's grave is situated on the north side of the church. It is very simple. The low headstone is undecorated and marked merely with his initials and the date of his death.

The zigzag which winds its way up the steep face of Selborne Hanger was cut by Gilbert White and his brother in 1753 to serve as a short cut to the summit of this high chalk hill. From the top there is a marvellous view and to the left of the path at this point is a rock, commonly known as the Wishing Stone, which was brought here from Farringdon by Gilbert White and his brothers.

Because the zigzag presents a stiff climb, this walk has been designed either to be done in its entirety or as two short strolls. Those merely wishing to enjoy the views from the top of the hanger should follow only the first four paragraphs of walking instructions and those who would prefer to avoid the climb may do so by ignoring paragraphs two, three and four.

It should be kept in mind that the area around Selborne is chalk and therefore inclined to be rather muddy after wet weather. Stout footwear is advisable.

20

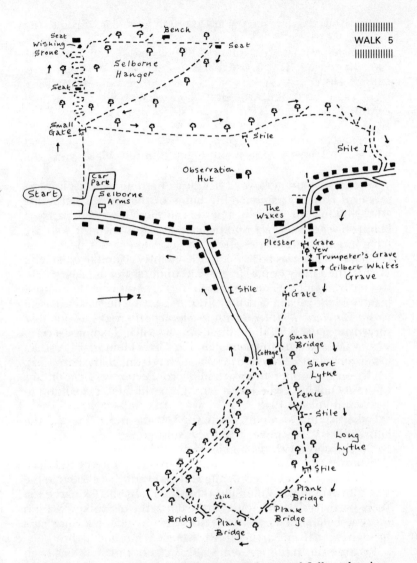

Turn off the A31 on to the B3006 at Alton and follow the signs to Selborne. Having entered the village turn right just beyond the Selborne Arms and park in the public car park at the rear of the building.

Leave the car park by the footpath that leads to the zigzag. This is on the left beside the entrance to the car park. It will bring you to a small gate in the fence at the edge of Selborne Common. Ignore a

21

footpath curving away to the left at this point and go through the gate.

Turn left to pass the National Trust sign on your right and climb the zigzag. (If you wish to miss this section of the walk, see A below.) Disregard a path that crosses this serpentine route at right-angles about halfway up, at a point where there is a seat, and continue the ascent. Near the top the path forks. Keep to the right-hand branch which will lead you to where the Wishing Stone and another seat are on your left. This is the viewpoint and it is worth pausing here to enjoy the beautiful view across the valley.

Leave the viewpoint by the way you entered it, passing the Wishing Stone on your right, and take the path which leads straight ahead towards the trees. Ignore any side turnings and keep the downward slope of the hanger on your right. Slowly the path widens and, after a short distance, appears to fork. The left-hand branch swings round to climb higher up the hillside so keep to the right which will soon lead you past a wooden bench on the left.

About 200 yards beyond this there is another seat, this time a metal one, sited slightly down the slope to the right. From here there is a good view of The Wakes in the valley. Turn sharp right on to a path leading down the hillside. This will bring you back to the National Trust sign at the foot of the zigzag. Turn sharp left.

(A — If you are joining the walk here, turn sharp right on to a path which skirts the fence on the right.) Almost immediately the wooden fence gives way to a wire one and at this point a reconstruction of Gilbert White's observation hut can be seen, surrounded by a protective fence, in the middle of the field to the right. Beyond it there is a good view of the rear of The Wakes.

Ignore a stile in the fence on the right and continue to follow the path along the base of the hanger. Where it forks keep to the right-hand branch. This will eventually bring you to where the path joins a wider one. Turn right on to this and follow it down the slope, passing a National Trust sign on your left, to reach a track.

Turn right on to the track which initially runs between high banks and then swings left. Ignore a stile in the fence to the right at this point and carry on to where the track joins the head of a short lane that leads to a T-junction. Turn right at the junction into a second lane and, ignoring a turning to the left, follow it round to the right. Disregard a footpath that leads up a bank to the right and another entering a field and keep to the lane, which will eventually bring you back to the B3006.

Having gone either slightly to the left or the right to gain better visibility, cross the road and take the path directly opposite the end of the lane. This leads up to the left-hand gate into the churchyard, passing the Old Vicarage on the left and the Plestor on the right. Beyond the gate the path passes the remains of the yew tree and the Trumpeter's grave on the left before skirting the south side of the church. At the far end of the building a narrow well-marked path leads to Gilbert White's grave, which is beside the far end of the east wall, and this makes a worthwhile short diversion.

To continue the walk follow the main path straight on across the graveyard to where it swings right beside the fence to reach a gate. Go through this and straight down the slope to the far corner of the field where a small bridge crosses a stream.

Beyond the bridge a path leads through the Short Lythe. It passes a cottage on the right and then follows the course of the stream for a short distance to where it is joined by another path that comes up the bank on the right. Ignore this and continue to follow the path straight ahead.

This will bring you to where a fence to keep out animals blocks the path. Beyond it a path descends a bank on the left and another begins at a stile. Ignore both of these, climb over the fence and keep to the main path which leads past a National Trust sign on the left and into Long Lythe.

Where the trees come to an end at the far end of Long Lythe there is a stile. Cross this and bear diagonally right down a slight slope to a plank bridge in the valley. Just beyond this the path crosses a second plank bridge and then leads on towards a lone oak tree.

Turn sharp right beside the tree to cross a third plank bridge and then walk straight ahead, keeping the hedge on your left. This will bring you to a stile in the corner of the field. Go over it and follow the narrow path round to the right. It crosses a bridge over a stream and then divides. Take the left-hand branch and, ignoring two minor turnings to the right, go up the slope to a track.

Turn right and follow the track through the wood. After a while the trees on the right end, giving good views of Long Lythe on the far side of the valley. Then the trees close in again.

Where the wood on the left ends, a track comes down the slope to converge with the main track. Ignore this and follow the main track round to the right.

Disregard another track that leads away to the right in the valley and carry straight on, passing a cottage on the right to reach the head of a lane. The lane leads up a sharp hill to join the road. Turn left to return to the Selborne Arms and the car park.

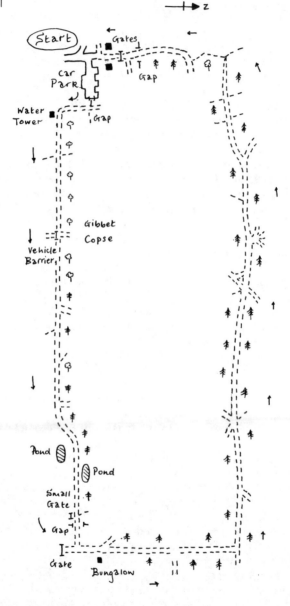

CHAWTON PARK WOOD

WALK 6

★

3 miles (4.5 km)

OS Landranger 186

This beautiful wooded area lies to the west of Alton. The old Pilgrim's Way which ran from Salisbury to Canterbury passed through it and it was once a favourite haunt of highwaymen. In an attempt to discourage their activities, a gibbet was erected here and the place where it stood is still known as Gibbet Copse.

Chawton Park Wood gets its name from the village of Chawton where Jane Austen spent the last eight years of her life. She died in 1817 at the early age of 41, just a few months before her last novel *Persuasion* was published.

In the days when Jane Austen was living in Chawton the woods were composed mainly of beech trees but today many of these old trees are gone, their place taken by stands of conifers planted by the Forestry Commission which purchased the area in 1949. The result is a wide expanse of mixed woodland that provides a habitat for a great variety of flora and fauna including many of the larger mammals such as deer.

It is these, together with the movements of Forestry Commission vehicles, that turn the woodland into a constantly changing network of narrow paths and faint tracks. For the purpose of clarity all such transitory thoroughfares have been ignored in the following text, the paths and tracks mentioned being the durable ones that form the commonly used routes through the wood.

Take the A31 from Alton to Four Marks and turn right just beyond Chawton End Garage into Boyneswood Road. This is signposted 'Medstead 1½'. Follow the road to where it swings sharp left and take a track on the right that leads to Chawton Wood car park.

Leave the car park by the gap at the far end and, ignoring a path straight ahead, turn right to follow a track which bends round to the left, passing a water tower on the right.

From here the track runs between a wood on the left and a fence on the right. This wood is Gibbet Copse. Ignore a path that

25

cuts across the track; a cross track which leads through a vehicle barrier on the right; a track to the left; two paths, one to the right and the other to the left; and a second grassy track on the left. Beyond this the track swings slightly left and eventually passes between two ponds, the first on the right behind the fence and the second beneath the trees on the left. Neither is large but, at the right time of the year, their surfaces are ablaze with a colourful display of flowers.

Not far from the ponds the track passes through a gap in a fence, at a point where there is a small gate on the right and a path to the left. Disregard both of these and continue along the track to the place where it meets another track in a T-junction. Turn left and walk past a white bungalow on the right. This will bring you to a point where the track divides.

Take the right-hand fork, which leads through the trees to a clearing on the brow of a hill. Go straight across it to reach another track on the far side and descend the slope to the valley.

Here the track meets a gravel one in a T-junction. Turn left on to this. It is almost immediately joined by a track from the right but disregard this and go straight on (passing another pair of tracks on the left, a path on the right, followed by a gravel track to the left with a minor track to the right and then a set of three tracks on the right) until you come to a place where the main track divides.

Take the left-hand fork. It runs up a slight slope and is crossed by two paths before eventually ending beside a fence at the edge of the wood.

Two narrow paths diverge from the end of the track. Take the one to the left. It runs along beside a fence on the right for a short distance before taking a slight detour through a gap in the fence and back again to avoid a fallen tree. Beyond this it carries straight on to join a track from the left.

Follow the track straight ahead to where it passes through a gap in a fence and joins a gravel one. Go through the gates straight ahead and, having passed between some houses, turn left into the car park.

HAMBLEDON

WALK 7

★

7½ miles (12 km)

OS Landranger 185 and 196

The village of Hambledon nestles amongst the high chalk hills to the north of Portsmouth where the western tip of the South Downs stretches into Hampshire. It is the largest village in the area and also one of the oldest.

Hambledon's main claim to fame was its cricket club. This was formed during the latter half of the 18th century and made a name for itself when it challenged and defeated an All-England team in 1770. Hambledon Cricket Club played on Broadhalfpenny Down to the north-east of the village. Here a granite monument marks the site of the original pitch.

This is a pleasant walk through rolling downland scenery but parts of it can be rather wet, especially when the crops are high, so it is advisable to wear waterproof footwear.

Take the A3(M) from Portsmouth travelling towards Petersfield and after 7 miles turn left at a junction marked Clanfield and Chalton. At the bottom of the slip road turn left again to follow the signs to Hambledon. Having entered the village pass the George Hotel on the left and the New Inn on the right; then park on the left.

Begin the walk by going back along the village street and turning right beside the George Hotel. This will bring you into a narrow lane which runs up a hill. Ignore a footpath to the right opposite Hill House and continue to follow the lane. Near the top of the hill it is joined by a narrow lane from the left but disregard this and carry straight on.

Not far beyond Rushmere Stud on the left there is a road junction. Turn left here and follow the lane past a cottage and some farm buildings on the right. Disregard a footpath to the right and, just beyond it, turn left on to a track marked 'Footpath'. The track curves right to pass the edge of a wood on the right. At this point it is joined by another track from the right but ignore it and keep to the main track which eventually swings left. Pass a stile set in the fence on the right and carry straight on to where the track meets a lane.

27

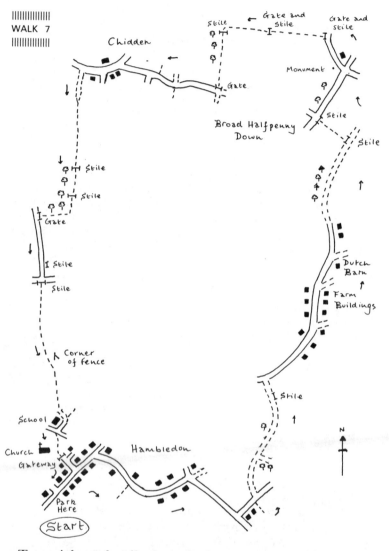

Turn right and walk along the lane passing Gliddens Farm House, some farm buildings and a track to the right. Just beyond this the lane leads through a farmyard. Go straight ahead ignoring a track to the right near the end of the farm buildings.

Disregard an unmetalled lane which joins the main one by a Dutch barn on the right and carry on to pass a house on the right. Just beyond this the lane becomes an unmetalled track. It runs between hedges for some distance before passing a wood on the

28

left and descending a slope. Near the bottom there is a stile in the fence on the left. Cross it and walk down the hillside to leave the field by another stile to reach the road.

Turn right to walk up the hill to the crossroads and turn left into Hyden Farm Lane. This will lead you past the cricket pitch and the monument on the left.

Continue to follow the road for another 100 yards and then turn left to cross a stile beside a field gate. Walk along the side of the field, keeping the fence on your left, and cross a second stile next to a gate at the far side. Carry straight on, still keeping the fence on your left until you come to the corner of a wood. Here there is a stile in the fence. Turn left to cross it and walk straight across the field to reach a gate at the far side, opening on to a lane.

Ignore a footpath straight ahead and turn right to follow the lane. It goes down a slope, at the bottom of which it is joined by a track to the right and a footpath to the left. Ignore these and another footpath on the right at the top of the next incline. Just beyond this there is a lane on the left but still keep to the main lane. It curves to the left at a point where it is joined by a second minor lane from the right and then passes a farm to reach a junction. This time bear right on to the lane marked 'Meonstoke 3¼ — Droxford 3¾'. Follow it up a slight hill and, as it bends right, turn left on to a track.

The track almost immediately narrows to a path which runs between bushes for some distance to reach a stile. Cross it and go straight ahead keeping the wood on your right. At the far side of the field there is a second stile and then eventually the wood on the right ends. Turn right to reach a field gate and then left on to a metalled track that leads to the road. Cross over to climb a stile on the opposite side and go straight up the hill, keeping the hedge on your left.

At the top the hedge ends. Bear slightly left to skirt the corner of a fence on your left and then head obliquely right towards a school in the valley. This will bring you to the head of a track which skirts the side of the playground and then curves right to run along the front of the building. Ignore a path that leads to the left at this point and carry on to where the track meets a lane.

Turn left and then almost immediately right into the churchyard. A path leads past the church to a gateway beyond which is a lane. Go straight down the lane to the road and turn right to reach the place where you parked your car.

SILCHESTER

WALK 8

★

5½ miles (8.5 km)

OS Landranger 175

Some of the most interesting Roman remains to be found in England are buried to the east of Silchester. There, beneath the fields, lie the remains of Calleva. This Roman city was built on a site originally fortified by the Celts. It was an extensive township covering some 235 acres and included amongst its buildings the oldest known Christian church in England. Yet today little is to be seen except the old city wall and the remains of the amphitheatre. The latter, which was once capable of holding 10,000 spectators, is situated outside the wall to the east of the city. It has been recently excavated and is well worth a visit.

On the eastern border of the Roman site and well away from the main complex of houses that form the village of Silchester, stands the present Silchester church. This is another place of interest. Dating from the 13th century, it contains a fine Jacobean pulpit and some medieval wall paintings.

The sites occupied by most Roman cities have developed into modern townships but Calleva did not and in this it is almost unique. Nobody knows why it died. It might have been merely because it failed to serve any useful pupose once the Romans left or it may have been due to some more dramatic cause such as plague.

Calleva means 'the town in the wood' and in Roman times it was surrounded by thick woodland which stretched westward from Kent. Today little of this remains but to the north of the village there is an area of pleasant woodland known as Benyon's Inclosure. It is bordered to the east by Mortimer West End, a small hamlet that lies right on the county boundary.

Take the A340 from Basingstoke travelling towards Aldermaston and turn right in Pamber Green on to the road to Little London. Where this ends in a T-junction turn left and follow the road for almost 2 miles to where The Calleva Arms is on the left. Turn left here to pass the cricket ground on your right and then take the first road on the right. Follow it for about 100 yards before turning left to park beside the beginning of a gravel

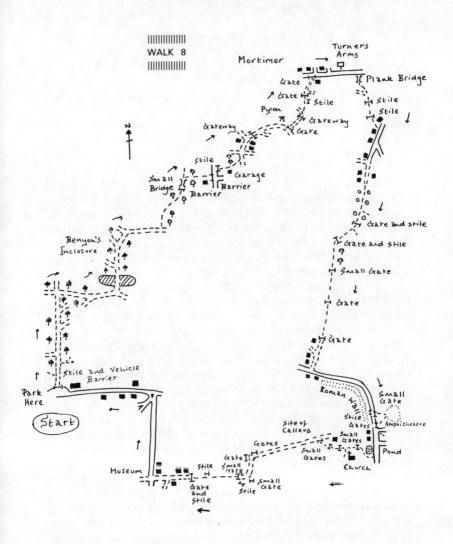

track, at a point where there are a pair of cottages called Heatherbrae and Firgate to the left of the road.

Cross the stile beside the vehicle barrier and follow the track ignoring a path to the left, another to the right and then a track to the left followed by two more to the right. This will bring you to a cross track. Turn right and, having passed another track on the right, continue to where the track forks.

Take the left-hand branch. This crosses a lake and then climbs a slope. Ignore a track to the left where the track swings right and then leave the main track as it swings left again to take one that leads straight ahead. Where this meets another track in a T-junction turn right and follow the fence on the left to its end. At this point a path, bordered by trees, leads away to the left. Turn left on to this. It quickly becomes narrower as it descends a slope through a wood then crosses a small bridge over a stream and divides. Take the right-hand branch. It leads up a tree-clad slope and passes a house on the right to reach the road.

Cross over, turn left and then almost immediately right where a stile gives access to a field. Follow the hedge on the right to a garage and, having passed it, turn left to head straight across the field, passing two small oak trees on your left. This will bring you to a track. Turn left and, ignoring a cross track, carry straight on, passing some farm buildings on the right, to reach the point where two tracks meet in a T-junction.

Turn right to pass the farmhouse on your right and follow the track through a gateway. Just beyond this the track divides. Keep to the left-hand branch which leads straight ahead down a slope towards some electricity pylons.

Beyond the pylons the track swings right and then divides. Take the left-hand fork which goes through a gate on the left. It climbs a slope to a gateway and then swings left. Leave it at this point and carry on up the hill keeping the fence on your right. This will bring you to another gate with a stile in the fence beside it. On the far side a track curves round to the right. Follow it straight ahead to reach some houses that border the road.

Cross over and turn right. This will lead you past The Turners Arms on the left to a place, about 100 yards beyond it, where a footpath leads over a plank bridge on the right. Recross the road at this point and follow the footpath as it twists left through some small trees and then turns right to skirt a field. Ignore an overgrown track on the right and continue to follow the hedge on the right to reach a stile where the hedge swings left. Cross this and go straight ahead to a second stile beyond which a path leads between houses to the road.

Turn right and follow the road to where it forks. Take the right-hand branch and, where the tarmac ends, continue to go straight ahead, ignoring a track to the right labelled 'Footpath'. Having passed some farm buildings on the right and a house on the left the track degenerates into a path that runs down a hill through bushes. Near the bottom it forks. Keep to the right-hand branch that leads on down the slope to a gate with a stile beside it. On the far side of this bear diagonally right, ignoring a narrow path which leads to a stile on the edge of a wood straight ahead, and walk across the field to another gate and stile. Beyond this a narrow path skirts the wood on the left.

At the end of this path there is a small gate. Go through it and follow the hedge on the right to reach a gate at the far side of the field, then follow the fence on the left across the brow of the hill to another gate in the corner of the next field. This opens on to a farmyard. Carry straight on, ignoring a track to the right beyond the first farm buildings, to reach the road and then turn left.

The road runs along beside the Roman city wall which can be seen over the hedge on the right. After some distance a stile gives access to it but ignore this and turn left just beyond it to go through a small gate on to the expanse of grass bordering the amphitheatre. The entrance to the amphitheatre is slightly to the right and, having visited it, a second small gate with a larger gate beside it set further along the hedge will bring you back to the road.

Ignore a lane and a footpath to the left at this point and follow the road round to the right. It crosses the head of another lane and, not far beyond this, the church of St Mary the Virgin is set back from the road on the right.

Turn right here and then bear right through the church car park, passing the pond on your right. This will bring you to a gate on the left that leads into the churchyard. Go through it and follow the path, ignoring a turning to the left at the far end of the church, to reach another small gate. Beyond this the path skirts some farm buildings on the right and leads through two more small gates to join a track.

Turn left. The track runs straight across the centre of what was once Calleva and a good idea of the size of the site can be gained from the city walls which can be seen across the fields on either side.

Ignore a pair of gates on the right and a gate straight ahead, where the track swings left at the far side of the city, and then another small gate to the left as it swings right again. Just beyond this the track ends at a point where there is a stile to the left and a path leading through a small gate straight ahead.

Take the path. It passes a stile set in the fence to the right and ends at a gate and stile that give access to a track. Follow this straight ahead, ignoring one turning to the left, to reach the road. Turn right to pass the Calleva museum on your right. This will bring you to a road junction. Cross over and take the road signposted 'Pamber Heath'. This is Kings Road and the place where you left the car is a few hundred yards along it on the right.

CHERITON

WALK 9

★

5 miles (8 km)

OS Landranger 185

On several occasions Cheriton has won the annual award for the best kept village in Hampshire and it is certainly one of the most beautiful in the county. It is situated on the banks of a small stream which is the beginning of the river Itchen. This rises in the hills to the south of the village and flows through Winchester and Eastleigh to join the sea at Southampton.

It was on the hills above Cheriton that one of the most important battles of the Civil War was fought. On 28th March 1644 Lord Hopton marched the Royalist army from Winchester to intercept the Roundheads who had been led into Hampshire by Sir William Waller. They met close to Cheriton Wood which Waller immediately occupied whilst Hopton did his best to dislodge him. The armies were well matched, having almost 10,000 men apiece, and the encounter lasted for several hours. It resulted in the Royalists being badly beaten and the slaughter was so great that the lanes are said to have run with blood.

The battle of Cheriton marked a turning point in the war. It was a defeat from which the Royalist army never recovered and which ultimately led to the downfall of King Charles I.

Take the B3046 from New Alresford to Cheriton and drive through the village to turn left at the war memorial. Park on the left by the village green.

Walk on along the lane, passing the green on your left and ignoring a footpath to the left marked 'The Itchen Way', and then bear left into a narrow lane marked 'No entry'. This will lead you up to the main road. Cross over and take the lane straight ahead, marked 'No through road'. Follow it for about 50 yards to pass a barn on the right and then turn right across a stile on to a grassy footpath. The footpath runs along beside a hedge on the right to a gate with a stile beside it. Cross this and continue to follow the hedge.

Within a short distance there is a gate in the hedge but ignore this and carry straight on. The path, which had become rather

34

indistinct, is now clearly visible again and the hedge on the right gives way to a fence with the narrow river Itchen on the far side of it.

Go straight ahead to reach a pair of stiles at the far end of the field and then carry on to reach a white fence at the far side of the next field. Here another stile gives access to a grassy path. It will lead you down to a lane passing a cottage on the left and the building that was once Cheriton Mill on the right.

Turn right to follow the lane to the road and cross over to take the track straight ahead. It leads up a slope to meet a second track in a T-junction. Turn right on to this track. Follow it to where it widens and divides, then take the left-hand fork. This will eventually bring you to a lane. Turn left to follow it. Where it swings left a track leads straight ahead but disregard this. Ignore a footpath which begins at a small gate on the left and carry straight on to reach a second track on the right.

Turn on to this and follow it up the slope. At the top it is joined by another track from the right and a footpath which leads through a small gate to the left, but ignore both of these and carry straight on.

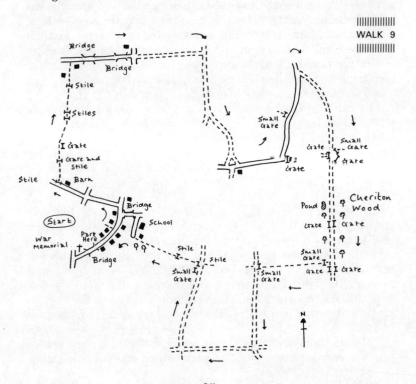

35

You are now in the area where the battle was fought in 1644. The track dips down to skirt Cheriton Wood on the left and a small pond on the right. Then, just as it enters the trees, it begins to climb again. Ignore a gate on the left marked 'Private' and another opposite it and continue to where the track emerges from the wood.

At this point there are field entrances on either side. Just before them a narrow path leads through the bushes on the right to a small gate. Turn right to follow this through the gate and then go straight ahead keeping the fence on your left. This will bring you to another small gate at the far side of the field. It opens on to a track with another path straight ahead.

Turn left on to the track and follow it to where four tracks meet, then turn right. Continue to where there is a path on the left and a track on the right, and then turn right again. The track leads up a slope between banks and at the top is joined by a path from the right at a point where there is a small gate and a stile on the left. Turn left to cross the stile and follow the narrow path to a second stile on the far side of the field.

Beyond this follow the hedge on the left to reach the beginning of a path that runs down the hillside between the hedge on the left and a fence on the right. This eventually emerges on to the end of a short lane. Turn right to pass the school on your right and then left over the bridge, on the far side of which turn left again to follow the lane back to the car.

PRESTON CANDOVER

WALK 10

★

4½ miles (7 km)

OS Landranger 185

Preston Candover is one of the three villages which take their names from the little Candover brook that joins the river Itchen near Alresford. It is larger than either Chilton Candover or Brown Candover and is set amongst the rolling chalk hills of central Hampshire.

Preston House, lying to the north of the village, was built during the early 18th century. It was the home of William Guiddott whose family originally came from Florence during the reign of Edward VI. Guiddott died not long after the house was completed and it was inherited by his nephew William Woodruffe. Since then it has been sold several times and is now the property of the Sainsbury family.

Moundsmere Manor is an attractive house situated to the north-west of Preston Candover. It is much younger than Preston House and was the home of Wilfred Buckley, who was a pioneer in clean milk production. A model dairy farm he built near the manor became quite famous in farming circles during the early part of this century.

Turn off the A31 in New Alresford on to the B3046 to Basingstoke. Follow this road to Preston Candover and drive through the village to park in the lay-by on the left just before the village hall.

Cross over and walk on along the road, passing the primary school on your right. This will take you out of the village. Ignore the road to Bradley on the right and carry straight on, passing the grounds of Preston House behind a fence on your left. Not far beyond this there is a drive on the right flanked by two gatehouses. It is marked 'Private Drive' but this is only to deter motorists. Turn right and follow it up the slope, from the top of which there are some good views across the hills to the right.

After this the drive goes on through a wood to the gates of Moundsmere Manor. In front of the gates it is joined by two tracks, one to the right and the other to the left. Take the

37

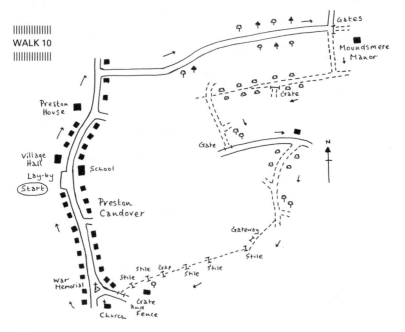

right-hand one. It will lead you past the manor house which is set back beyond a field on the left.

The track leads down into a valley and swings right at a point where it is joined by another track from the left. Ignore this and continue along the main track. Within a short distance it divides. Take the right-hand fork which goes straight ahead through some bushes and gradually narrows to a path.

Where the path is crossed by a track, turn left. The track climbs a slope and is joined by a track from the left near the corner of a wood. Disregard this and carry straight on, passing the wood on your left to reach the place where the track meets the road. Turn left and follow the verge to where the road swings right and there is a cottage on the left. Cross the road at this point and turn sharp right on to a track marked 'Right of Way'.

The track runs for some distance through bushes and then emerges at a point where it is met by another track from the right. Still go straight on keeping the trees on your left. From here Preston House can be seen in the valley to the right.

Where the wood on the left ends and a grassy track leads away to the left, leave the main track to follow the hedge on the right. It curves right and is then broken by a field gateway. Ignore this and carry on along the hedge to a stile. Go over this and head straight across the field to a second stile. Beyond this go straight ahead again to cross a third stile and then follow the fence on the right.

38

This will bring you to a gap in the fence in the corner of the field. Go through it and continue to skirt the fence on the right.

The next stile is situated between a large ash tree and the fence. It gives access to the last field, at the far side of which a stile enables you to reach a stable yard. There is a gate straight ahead with a two bar fence beside it. Climb over this fence and turn right to follow the road. Go right again at the junction, passing the War Memorial on your left, and walk along the road to the lay-by, which is on the left.

HANNINGTON

WALK 11

★

5 miles (8 km)

OS Landranger 174 and 185

Hannington is a delightful little village set high on a hill in the northern part of the county not far from the Berkshire border. It is surrounded by rolling countryside which affords magnificent views. Parts of the area are used for farming but large sections have been set aside for training racehorses from local stables.

In Saxon times these hills had a very different use. They were a royal hunting ground. William the Conqueror exchanged it for land in Winchester on which to build a castle but even after this transaction the English kings still continued to hunt here. King John in particular was a frequent visitor to the area.

Leave Basingstoke on the A339 travelling towards Newbury and drive into Kingsclere to take the B3051 which is signposted 'Overton 6'. Follow this for 1½ miles to where Whitehill car park is on the left.

Walk back to the road and turn sharp left on to a path which has a field entrance on the right. This leads through bushes to a gate at a point where there is another gate and a stile on the left. Go through the gate straight ahead and follow the path up the slope, keeping the fence on your right. This will bring you to another gate, beyond which the path eventually joins a lane.

Turn left and then almost immediately right on to a lane signposted 'Walkeridge Farm'. Leave this where it turns right at the farm and go straight ahead, passing the farm buildings on your right, to reach a gate with a small gate beside it.

Go through the small gate and follow the hedge on the left, passing through two fields to reach the bottom of the slope. Here there is another combination of gates opening on to a track. Turn left and follow the track, ignoring another track which almost immediately branches off to the left.

At the top of the hill the track is joined by a grassy track from the left. Disregard it and carry straight on to the top of the next slope where the track swings left. Leave it at this point to take a footpath that leads through a small gate straight ahead. Ignore a

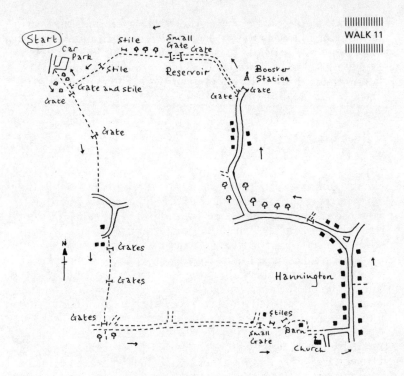

stile that gives access to a field on the left and follow the fence round to the left, passing a second stile on the left. Beyond this the path twists round behind a barn on the right to join a drive.

Turn left to walk along the drive to the road, passing Hannington church on the right, then go straight ahead. This will take you past the village green on your right to a T-junction. Turn left to follow the road through the village, ignoring a footpath on the right. Where the road turns right by The School House on the right and is joined by a lane from the left, turn left.

Follow the lane until you eventually come to the place where it divides. Take the right-hand fork which is marked 'Private Road to Freemantle Park Farm'. The lane leads downhill through a wood then passes some houses before climbing a slope to a booster station. Bear left beside the entrance to this on to a track that goes through a gate.

The track curves to the left through a stand of trees and then passes Cottington Hill Reservoir on the left to reach another gate. Go through this to a small gate straight ahead and then follow the path that leads along the edge of the wood.

41

Ignore a stile on the right where the wood ends and carry straight on, following the fence on the left to reach another stile in the corner of the field. Carry straight on across the next field to reach a gate and stile in the far corner and then turn right to follow the path back through the bushes to the road and the car park, which is on the right.

FAWLEY DOWN

WALK 12

★

4 miles (6 km)

OS Landranger 185

Fawley Down is an expanse of open countryside to the east of
Winchester. Its softly rolling hills provide magnificent views,
especially in the area around Cheesefoot Head where the Devil's
Punch Bowl lies at the foot of the northern slope. This is a natural
amphitheatre formed by the curve of the hill and, although it is
not as big as its namesake at Hindhead in neighbouring Surrey, it
is every bit as beautiful.

Most of the land in this part of Hampshire is used for arable
farming and in recent years both Fawley Down and the Devil's
Punch Bowl have gained a new claim to fame for it is here that
some of the county's most impressive crop circles have appeared.

Should you be lucky enough to spot one of these mysterious
phenomena, please do not wander into the growing crops
without the farmer's permission.

Turn off the A31 just east of Winchester on to the A272 to
Petersfield. Follow this road for a little over a mile to the top of
Telegraph Hill and park in the car park on the left at Cheesefoot
Head.

Leave the car park, turn right and walk along the verge for a short
distance to reach a small gate on the right. From here there is an
excellent view of the Devil's Punch Bowl in the valley. Do not go
through the gate but turn left beside it to cross the road and take a
track marked 'South Downs Way' that leads through a gate with a
small gate beside it.

At the far side of the field this track swings right at a point
where it is joined by two bridleways, one to the left and the other
straight ahead. Take the one that goes straight ahead. It runs
along the top of the hill and affords magnificent views across the
open fields to the left.

Where the ridge ends the track swings left and is joined by
another from the right. Ignore this and follow the track round to
the left. It leads down a slope, skirting some army ranges hidden
behind a hedge on the right.

43

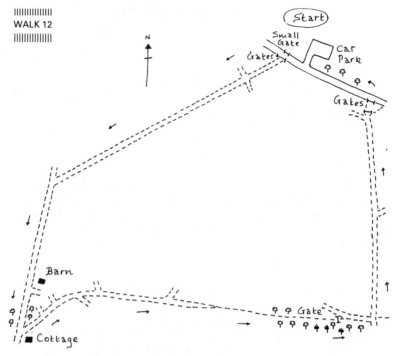

Ignore a track to the left just beyond a barn and carry on through a short belt of trees to where the track merges with another from the left. Turn sharp left on to this, passing a cottage garden on the right. Disregard two tracks to the left and where the main track forks take the left-hand branch which goes straight ahead. Ignore a turning to the left and follow the main track down into the valley where it forks again. This time take the right-hand branch. It leads up a slope between hedges.

Near the top of the slope the hedge on the right gives way to a fence and the track narrows to a path. For a short distance there are good views and then the path becomes tree lined and leads through bushes to skirt a wood on the right. It then goes through a gate and merges with a track from the left.

Go straight on for a short distance to where the track meets another in a T-junction and a path leads straight ahead. Turn left to follow the track. It runs between open fields and once again there are excellent views. Ignore a bridleway to the right and carry on to where there is another bridleway to the left and two sets of gates straight ahead. Go through the gates to reach the road and turn left. This will bring you back to the car park which is on the right.

44

CALSHOT

WALK 13

★

3 miles (4.5 km)

OS Landranger 196

Calshot lies south of Fawley on the western side of the entrance to Southampton Water. It has a wide shingle beach and good views of the Isle of Wight and many interesting vessels can be seen making their way to and from Southampton docks.

The marshland which is protected by the spit of land projecting into the harbour mouth has been set aside as a conservation area by the County Council. The public are not allowed to enter the marshes but even from the path it is possible to enjoy the wide variety of bird life inhabiting them.

Take the A326 from Southampton to Fawley and, having passed Fawley Refinery on the left, follow the signs to Calshot. After 1½ miles turn right opposite Fawley Power Station on to the road signposted 'Lepe 2¾'. This is Stanswood Road. Drive along it for just under 200 yards and then turn right on to a gravel track. Park on the right near where the track meets the road.

Start the walk by turning left to follow Stanswood Road back to the T-junction and then turn right. This will lead you past Fawley Power Station and some farm buildings on the left. Continue along the road until you come to a garage on the right and then turn left to cross a stile beside a field gate. Walk straight ahead following the fence on the right. This will bring you to a plank bridge and then a stile with another small bridge beyond it. Cross these and follow the path which swings left and then right passing Fawley Power Station. This will bring you to where the path meets another in a T-junction at the edge of the marsh.

Turn right and follow the path. It runs between a fence on the right and the marsh on the left. Eventually the fence on the right veers away from the path. Just beyond this point there is a grassy path to the right. Ignore it and carry straight on to reach the road and turn right.

The road runs past a car park on the left. At the far end of this turn left and then right to go round the beach huts and follow the line of short wooden posts which reinforce the shoreline.

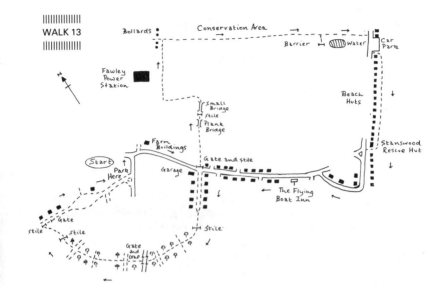

Continue to follow the shore to where the posts end and Stanswood Rescue hut is on the right. Turn right here to regain the road and then left, ignoring a road marked 'No entry' that leads straight ahead.

The road climbs a slight slope and swings right. Ignore a turning to the right and carry straight on. This will lead you past The Flying Boat Inn on the left.

When you come to a garage on the left, turn left just before it on to an unmetalled track called Elmfield Lane. This goes past some houses and then degenerates into a path that leads to a stile. Cross this and bear right to follow the path through the trees to a clearing. Ignore one path to the right and another to the left and follow the main path straight ahead. After a short distance it is crossed by a track and then leads on to reach a gap in a fence that gives access to the road.

Cross straight over to go through a similar gap beside a gate on the opposite side and then follow the path straight ahead. It is crossed by a track but ignore this and carry straight on.

The path crosses a valley and then enters some more trees where it is crossed by a path. Still go straight ahead and continue across a track to reach a stile at the far side of the wood. Go over this and head straight across the field towards a gate on the far side. A little to the left of the gate is a stile which gives access to a track. Turn right and, ignoring a footpath to the left and another to the right a little further on, follow the track to the car.

LONGPARISH

WALK 14

★

3 miles (4.5 km)

OS Landranger 185

As its name suggests, Longparish village is very elongated. It stretches for almost a mile along the road which runs through the Test valley from Forton to Hurstbourne Priors. Parts of it are very pretty. There are several delightful thatched cottages and a lovely manor house backing on to the river.

The section of the river Test skirting Longparish has a beauty all of its own. It is very popular with fishermen for it is here that some of the biggest trout are to be caught.

Turn off the A303 3 miles east of Andover on to the road signposted 'Longparish 1 — B3048'. Drive along this for 1½ miles and then turn left just opposite the Cricketer's Inn into North Acre. Follow the road round to the left and park.

Return to the main road through the village and turn first left and then almost immediately right by the bus stop on the right to cross a stile in a fence set back from the road. Bear left to follow the footpath across the field, passing the end of a fence on your left. This will bring you to a second stile in the corner of the field beyond which a footbridge over the river gives access to another stile. From here there are good views of Longparish House to the left.

Ignore a stile to the right and turn left to walk along a low bank that crosses the field. This will bring you to a small plank bridge beyond which the path swings right to skirt the fence.

In the corner of the field there is a stile. Cross it and go straight ahead to reach another at the far side of the next field. Beyond this a plank bridge over a stream gives access to the river bank where a path runs along beside the water to reach the old mill. Go through the vehicle barrier at the end of this path, turn left to pass the mill on your right and then follow the lane to the road. Turn left to walk along the side of the road until you come to the gates of Longparish House on the left. Just beside them a stile gives access to a field. Go over it and follow a narrow path to a second stile set in the wall by the gates at the far side. Cross this and turn

47

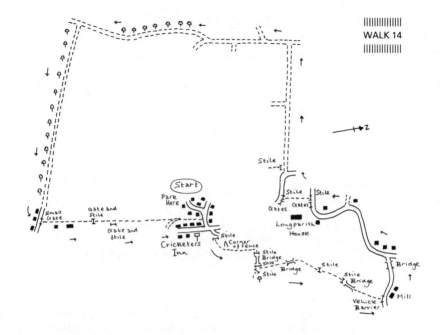

right to follow the road to the corner. Here, as the road swings right, a track leads straight ahead. Take the track and, ignoring a footpath which crosses a stile to the left, follow it up the hill. Near the top it is joined by another, rather overgrown track from the left but disregard this and carry straight on to reach the place where the track meets a wider one in a T-junction.

Turn left here and follow the track through the fields, ignoring one turning to the right and another to the left. This will bring you to where the track divides. Take the right-hand fork. It skirts a small wood on the right and then swings right to descend a slope.

At the bottom it is joined by a track from the left signposted 'Footpath'. Turn left on to this. For some distance it is bordered by a line of trees on the right and where these end it meets the head of a metalled lane. Continue along this for about 25 yards and then turn left through a gate into a field.

Follow the fence on the right to where the garden ends and then head straight across the field to reach a gate with a stile beside it. Cross the stile and follow the path straight ahead.

Ignore a stile by a gate on the right and carry on to where the path meets a track. Follow this straight ahead. It quickly narrows to a path which runs between gardens to reach the road. This is North Acre. Turn left and then left again to reach your car.

FARLEY MOUNT

WALK 15

★

6 miles (9.5 km)

OS Landranger 185

Farley Mount Country Park is situated on the high chalk hills to the west of Winchester. It is an area of great natural beauty and magnificent views. From some places it is possible to see right across Hampshire to the hills around Salisbury and from others Southampton is visible on the horizon.

Farley Chamberlayne church is an interesting early Norman building standing in the fields at some distance from the nearest village. It is approached through an avenue of lime trees that were planted in 1922 as a memorial to the local men who died during the First World War. In the vestry is a beacon that dates back to the reign of Edward III. It was used on Beacon Hill to alert those living in the area when danger threatened. The church also contains several memorials to members of the St John family. This family, which was closely related to Henry VII, once owned the land here but their home has vanished long ago.

The monument on Beacon Hill, the highest part of Farley Mount, was erected during the 18th century by Sir Paulet St John to the memory of a horse that saved his life. Whilst out hunting one day he came upon a chalk pit so suddenly that he could not stop. The horse leapt into the pit, which was over 20 ft deep, and landed without injury either to itself or its rider.

Take the A3090 from Hursley travelling towards Winchester and just over 1 mile beyond the village turn left on to a lane signposted 'Farley Mount 2¾ — Sparsholt 3'. Take the first lane on the left and follow it to the T-junction. Turn right here and then immediately left into the car park.

Return to the road and turn right to reach the junction. Cross over and go straight ahead through a gate that opens on to a track. After a while the track narrows to a path and runs between bushes to emerge at the side of a field. From a gateway on the right there is a good view of the monument on Beacon Hill. Pass this gateway and carry straight on to follow the path through some more bushes.

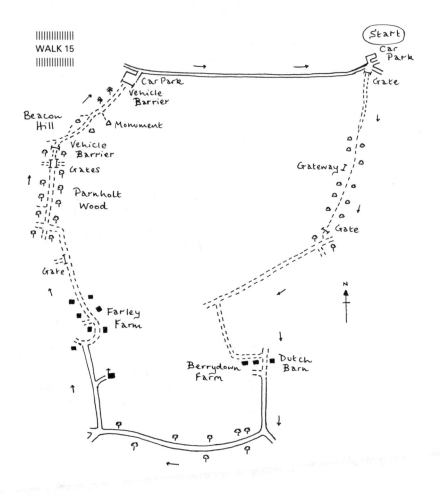

Where the path leaves the bushes walk straight ahead to reach a gate. Go through it and bear first left and then right on to a track. The track is almost immediately joined by another from the left but ignore it and carry straight on. After some distance there is a second track to the left. Turn left here.

The track, which can be rather muddy in places, leads to a farm, where it swings left to pass the farmhouse and a barn on the right before meeting another track in a T-junction. Turn right on to this, passing a Dutch barn on your left beyond which the track becomes metalled and leads to a lane. Turn right to follow the lane up the hill and then carry on to the crossroads.

Turn right here on to the no through road to Farley church. After some distance it forks. The right-hand branch leads through the avenue of lime trees to the church and the left-hand branch goes on to a farm.

To continue the walk take the left-hand branch and where it forks again bear right and then left to pass through the farmyard to a track that leads straight ahead. Ignore a track going towards an aircraft hanger at the far side of a field on the left and carry straight on to where the track enters the wood. At this point it is crossed by another track. Turn right and walk through the trees, ignoring a bridleway to the left and a grassy cross track that goes through gates on either side of the track you are following.

Eventually the track passes through a vehicle barrier and emerges from the wood. It is joined by a path from the left and swings right to follow the crest of the hill. From here there are magnificent views to the left. Ignore a path which diverges from the track where the fence on the left ends and carry straight on. The track leads through some bushes and then is joined by a path from the left. Just beyond this a path to the right leads up to the Beacon Hill monument. This makes a worthwhile diversion, not only to see the monument but also to enjoy the beautiful views.

After visiting the monument return to the track and follow it on down the slope and through the car park to the road. Turn right to walk along the road to the junction and the car park where you left your car.

THE BISHOP'S PURLIEU

WALK 16

★

3 miles (4.5 km)

OS Landranger 196

The area of wood and heathland to the south-east of Lyndhurst is one of the most beautiful parts of the New Forest. There are magnificent views to be seen here as well as several features of interest.

To the south of the Beaulieu Road lies the Bishop's Purlieu, a stretch of bog approximately 1 mile in length and ½ mile wide surrounded by a medieval earthwork known as Bishop's Dyke. The area which the earthwork encloses is said to have been a piece of church land granted to the Bishop of Winchester by the King.

According to an old story the King promised to give the Bishop as much land in the forest as he could crawl round on his hands and knees in a day. It is possible that by this method he had not thought to lose much but the Bishop was an active man and managed to crawl right round an area which provided some of the best opportunities for hunting snipe to be found in the forest. This is a good story but not necessarily a true one. The very fact that the shape of the Bishop's Dyke is so irregular tends to belie it and it is possible that the dyke was merely built to enclose a fish pond.

Take the B3056 from Lyndhurst travelling towards Beaulieu and after 3 miles turn right just before the bridge over the railway line to enter Shatterford car park.

Go through the traffic barrier at the rear of the car park and where the pine trees end turn right on to a grassy track that skirts the trees. After a short distance it cuts through a group of trees and merges with another track from the right. Follow this to the left. It crosses a small bridge over the marsh and then swings to the right. This marsh is part of the Bishop's Purlieu.

The track crosses an area of open heathland and then divides. Keep to the left-hand fork and where this splits three ways as it enters the trees still keep to the left. The track runs through the edge of the wood and is joined by a path from the left opposite a clearing on the right. Ignore this and follow the track down a slope.

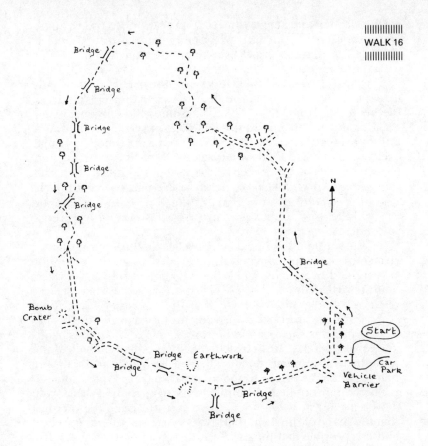

Just over the brow of the hill it narrows to a path and veers slightly to the left. It then swings right again near the bottom of the slope and winds through the trees to emerge from the wood. Ignore a path leading straight ahead and bear right to re-enter the trees. Here the path curves slightly left again to reach a clearing. Go straight across it and through a clump of trees to a larger clearing with a bridge on the left.

Cross the bridge and follow the path as it curves to the left over two more bridges. Beyond this it widens to skirt the trees on the right and, after some distance, crosses a bridge and leads through a group of trees to another bridge. On the far side of this it divides. Take the left-hand fork, which is the wider of the two and curves to the right almost immediately to enter a small wood.

As it emerges from the trees it widens into a track. Ignore a path which diverges from it to the right and another that leads away to the left and keep to the track until, having passed a bomb crater on the right, it comes to a point where four tracks meet. Turn left to follow a track through another small wood.

At the far side the track merges with a grassy one from the right and swings left to cross two bridges over the marsh. It then leads up a slight slope and cuts through a low earthwork. This is part of the medieval Bishop's Dyke that surrounds the Purlieu.

Carry straight on, ignoring a turning to the right that leads to a railway bridge. The track descends a slope to cross another bridge over the marsh and then swings left to skirt a line of fir trees on the left. Where it forks keep to the left-hand branch. This will take you back to the vehicle barrier at the rear of the car park.

LONGSTOCK

WALK 17

★

6½ miles (10 km)

OS Landranger 185

The pretty little village of Longstock lies in the Test valley to the north of Stockbridge. It contains several delightful thatched cottages and near Longstock House, to the north of the village, are some water gardens which are often open to the public during the summer months.

In the Dark Ages the area around Longstock was frequented by Danish invaders who made their way up the river Test in their small ships. They had a dock at Longstock where they would stop to refurbish their craft before returning to the sea. It was near here, at Andover, that King Ethelred made his first payment of Danegeld to Olaf the Dane.

To the west of Longstock is Danebury Hill. In spite of its name this is an Iron Age hillfort. It is the finest of its kind in Hampshire with a triple ring of ramparts encompassing 13 acres.

Yet it is not only its history that makes this area interesting. On the high ground to the east of Longstock there is a radio telescope and good views of this may be obtained on several parts of the walk.

Take the A3057 from Stockbridge travelling towards Andover and after ¼ mile turn left on to a lane signposted 'Longstock ½'. The lane crosses the river and ends in a T-junction in Longstock village. Turn left and then right by the church. Park on the left just opposite a cemetery on the right.

Walk back past the church and turn left to take the road running through the village. Ignore the turning to the right by The Peat Spade Inn and carry straight on to where the road turns sharp left. Leave it at this point to take a track leading straight ahead.

The track is fairly short and ends at a gate. Go through this and follow the hedge on the right to a stile in the far corner of the field. Cross the stile and continue to follow the hedge. This will bring you to a second stile. Cross it and go on along the hedge until you come to a small gate on the right. Pass through this and turn sharp left to reach a gate in the corner of the field. This opens on to a track that leads to the road.

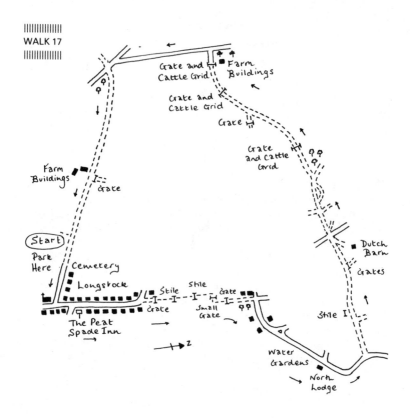

Turn right to follow the verge. It will lead you past the grounds of Longstock House on the left and gives views of the radio telescope straight ahead. After about ½ mile Longstock Water Gardens are hidden behind a hedge on the right.

Having passed a cottage called North Lodge on the right, continue along the road for about ¼ mile and then turn left on to a track marked 'Byway' at a point where the road curves right. The track runs through a valley and, at the beginning, can be rather muddy in places. Ignore a track to the right and then a stile in the fence to the left. Beyond this a grassy track goes through a pair of gates to the right but still carry straight on until you eventually come to where the track you are following merges with another from the right and joins the road.

Cross over and take the wide track straight ahead. This divides almost immediately so keep to the left-hand branch. It will lead you past a short track which goes to a field on the right and a grassy track that skirts a field on the left. Just beyond this the track appears to divide again but the two branches soon rejoin.

Where the track divides yet again, keep to the left-hand fork. It skirts a wood on the right and then crosses a cattle grid with a gate beside it. Beyond this the track runs between fields and there are good views of Danebury hillfort on the horizon straight ahead. The track is joined by another from the left marked 'Private Road' and then crosses two more cattle grids with gates beside them before passing some farm buildings on the right to reach the road.

Turn left and follow the road up the hill to the T-junction, then turn left and sharp left again on to a track marked 'Byway' which passes some trees on the right. The track leads over the brow of a hill and then passes some farm buildings on the right. Just beyond this a track leads away through a field gate on the left but ignore it and carry straight on. There are now more good views of the radio telescope to the left as the byway descends the slope.

Disregard a footpath to the right and carry straight on where the track becomes a metalled lane. This runs down past the cemetery and to the place where you parked the car.

BROCKENHURST

WALK 18

★

8 miles (12.5 km)

OS Landranger 196

This walk is set in one of the most environmentally varied areas of the New Forest and is of particular interest to the nature lover. The first half of the route leads across open heathland and through dense coniferous woods where walkers may be lucky enough to catch a glimpse of the timid Japanese sika deer. These creatures, once regarded as sacred animals in their native country, have white rumps and white spotted coats. They were originally kept in captivity by Lord Montagu on his estate at Beaulieu but, in 1904, a pair escaped. The following year he released another pair to join them and now there are about 60 living wild in the woods.

The second half of the walk passes through Roydon Woods Nature Reserve, an area mainly composed of mixed deciduous woodland, which is cared for by the Hampshire and Isle of Wight Naturalists' Trust to whom it was donated by Mr P Barker-Mill in 1978. It contains a wide variety of flora and fauna including red deer, badgers, buzzards and a vast range of flowering plants.

William Gilpin, the famous author and naturalist, was once the minister of Boldre church. His book *Scenery of the New Forest* was one of the most popular works on natural history written during the 18th century. Gilpin is buried in Boldre churchyard where his grave can be seen to the north of the church.

Brockenhurst church is the only forest church mentioned in the Domesday Book. In its churchyard are a group of graves dating back to the First World War and also the grave of another famous New Forest personality, Brusher Mills.

Brusher Mills, who gained his nickname from the careful way in which he swept the Balmer Lawn cricket pitch between innings, made his living as a snake catcher. The snakes were sold to London Zoo where they were used to feed the king cobras. He was very quick and deft in his work and could pick up an adder in his bare hands without getting bitten.

Balmer Lawn is one of the open grassy areas which are such a common feature of the New Forest. It once served as a race

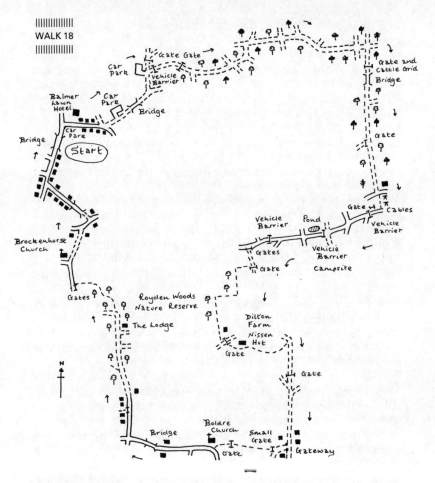

course where New Forest pony races were held. On its edge is the Balmer Lawn Hotel. This was the operational headquarters used by General Eisenhower and General Montgomery prior to the liberation of France in the Second World War.

Although dogs are, of course, permitted on this walk, they should be kept under strict control particularly in the holiday camp and the nature reserve. Walkers are also asked to keep to the tracks and paths in the reserve and not to pick or damage any of the flowers and plants.

Take the A337 from Lyndhurst to Brockenhurst and, on the outskirts of the village, turn left just beyond the Balmer Lawn Hotel on to the road signposted 'Beaulieu 6 — B3055'. Park in Balmer Lawn car park on the right just beyond the turning.

Leave the car park and turn right to walk along the B3055 passing Balmer Lawn Hotel on your left. Where the buildings on the left end and the road swings right, take a track which leads straight ahead, ignoring another to the left signposted 'Private Properties Only'. The track runs past Tilery Road car park on the left and over a bridge, some distance beyond which it divides. Take the left fork. It is marked 'Car park 150 yards'.

Ignore a track that leads through a gate beside Standing Hat car park and turn right on to a second track. Beyond the vehicle barrier this swings to the right, passes through a gate and is joined by another track from the right. Disregard this and carry straight on ignoring all side turnings.

Where the track is crossed by another gravel one, still go straight ahead keeping to the main track until you come to a second major junction where two gravel tracks cross. Turn right here and follow the track through the gate and over the bridge which crosses the railway line. Ignore one track to the left and another to the right and carry straight on until you come to the road.

Cross over and follow the line of electricity cables to a metalled track bordering a campsite, then turn right. Ignore a gate to the right and a track to the left and continue to where the metalled track meets another in a T-junction. Turn left and then almost immediately right to pass a chemical closet emptying point on the left.

Where the track is crossed by an unmetalled one go straight on, passing the pond on your right. This will bring you to a place where the track is crossed by a second coming from the entrance to the campsite. Go straight over this and on along the track marked 'Overflow campsite'.

As the track curves left leave it and follow the one straight ahead through the vehicle barrier. It passes the remains of a track to the right just beyond which there is a turning to the left. Go left here, passing through the smaller of the two gates to reach another gate straight ahead. Turn right beside it and then sharp left on to a path marked 'Bridleway' that runs between fences with a wood to the right.

At the corner of the wood the path turns to the right and then left again to skirt Roydon Woods Nature Reserve on the right and eventually reach a farm. Here it is crossed by a track but ignore this and carry straight on to pass some nissen huts on the left. Beyond this the path ends at a second track.

Turn right and follow the track which runs for some distance between fields to reach a gate. Here it is joined by another track from the right. Ignore it and another to the left and go straight on until you reach a place where there is a pair of houses and some farm buildings on the left and a wooden machinery shed on the right with a thatched farmhouse beside it.

Turn right to go through a gateway between the shed and the farmhouse. As the track swings left to enter the grounds of the house, go through a small wooden gate straight ahead and follow the path, keeping the fence on your left. At the far end of the field another, larger gate opens on to a track which leads straight ahead, passing Boldre churchyard on the right. This is the churchyard where William Gilpin is buried and it is worth pausing here to find his grave.

Where the track joins the lane, turn right. The lane goes steadily downhill, is joined by another lane from the left and crosses the Lymington river before climbing a slight slope to a crossroads. Turn right here onto the lane marked 'No through road'. Ignore a bridleway that leads through a gate to the left just beyond Myrtle Cottage and continue along the lane to pass a farm on the right. Beyond this the lane becomes a track that leads through Roydon Woods Nature Reserve. Follow it to where, having passed a cottage called 'The Lodge' on the right, it climbs a slope and swings left. At this point it is joined by a path going straight ahead.

Take the path. It skirts some fields on the right and then winds its way through woodland before cutting between more fields to reach the road. Turn right to follow the road to Brockenhurst church where Brusher Mills is buried. To find his grave take the path behind the church leading down into the churchyard. The war graves are on the right and Brusher Mills' grave is between them and the path.

The walk continues along the track which runs down a slope passing the churchyard on the left. Where this track joins a road turn right and then almost immediately left by the lodge gates on to another track leading to a footbridge over the railway. Cross the bridge and take the lane straight ahead to reach the road. Turn right to follow the road out of Brockenhurst. The car park is on the right just beyond the bridge over the river.

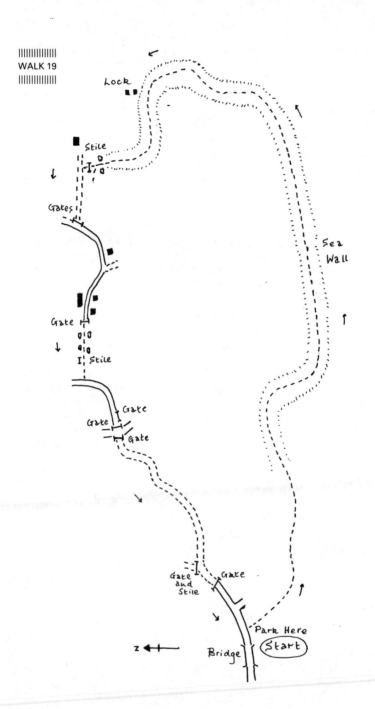

||||||||||||
WALK 19
||||||||||||

Lock

Stile

Gates

Sea
Wall

Gate

Stile

Gate
Gate
Gate

Gate
and
Stile

Gate

Park Here

Start

z

Bridge

KEYHAVEN

WALK 19

★

3½ miles (5.5 km)

OS Landranger 196

This is a pleasant coastal walk which provides beautiful views of the Solent and the Isle of Wight. Parts of it run along the edge of marshland where a wide variety of birdlife is to be seen and in other places there are good views of the small craft that frequent the Lymington river.

Hurst Castle stands at the end of a narrow spit of land stretching out from Keyhaven towards the Isle of Wight. The castle was built by Henry VIII as part of his coastal defences at a time when he was expecting an invasion from France. Today little of the original building can be seen for it is almost completely enclosed by two extensions added during the reign of Queen Victoria.

For a short period in the 17th century Charles I was imprisoned in Hurst Castle. He was brought here from Carisbrooke Castle on the Isle of Wight in November 1648 but was soon moved to Windsor and from there to London for his trial.

Take the A337 from Christchurch travelling towards Lymington. After 4 miles turn on to the B3058 to Milford on Sea. Follow this road for 3½ miles and then turn right again on to a road signposted 'Keyhaven 1'. Drive straight through the village passing the war memorial on your left and, just before The Gun inn on the right, turn left on to a 'No through road'. Within a short distance this road crosses a bridge just beyond which there are parking spaces on the right. However, should these be full, as in summer they often are, there is alternative parking in the public car park opposite The Gun and you should then start the walk by returning to the bridge.

The parking spaces at the far side of the bridge border the harbour wall and where this swings right a narrow path leads away beside the water. Turn right on to this and follow it along the side of the harbour. From here there are good views of Hurst Castle straight ahead.

After a short distance the path swings left and skirts the tide line for a while before swinging slightly right and then left to mount the low wall that separates the sea from the salt marshes on the left. For those interested in ornithology this will prove to be the best part of the walk. The elevated pathway provides excellent views across the marshes which invariably teem with birds.

As the wall swings right again the marshes give way to fields and the views of the Isle of Wight are even better. Continue along the path until, having swung left to border the mouth of the Lymington river, it swings left once more passing a lock on the right.

From here the path leads along the bank of an inlet which swings right and then ends. At this point there is a house facing the water. The path runs through some bushes and then swings slightly left at a place where there is a stile in the hedge on the right. Cross the stile from where a narrow path leads to the drive, then turn left and walk down the drive to the lane.

Turn left again to follow the lane. Ignore a track leading to a footpath on the left and carry on along the lane until you come to the end. Here a gate straight ahead opens on to a gravel footpath.

The path runs for some distance through bushes and, where it emerges from them, there is a stile on the right. Ignore it and carry straight on to reach a lane and then turn left.

This will bring you to a place where the tarmac ends. There is a gate on the left and another straight ahead. Go through the one straight ahead, cross a track just beyond it and take an unmetalled track that leads through a gate on the far side.

The track winds between fields for some distance before being joined by another track that comes through a high gate on the right. This gate has a stile beside it marked 'Footpath' but ignore it and continue along the main track. It passes through a gate and becomes metalled, then leads on to cross the bridge by the parking area.

21/10/18 GOOD WALK CRISP BUT ALLOVER SUN SHINE LUNCH @ FURZEY GDNS

MINSTEAD

WALK 20

★

3 miles (4.5 km)

OS Landranger 195

Minstead is situated near the northern edge of the New Forest. It is a pretty village with many interesting features including an ancient church, the grave of a famous author, some beautiful gardens and a public house with a very interesting name.

The 13th century church is constructed of wattle and daub with a lime coating. It is a most unusual shape and has a three tier pulpit. Beneath a large oak tree in the rear of the churchyard is the grave of Sir Arthur Conan Doyle, the creator of Sherlock Holmes. The author, who also had a house in the nearby village of Brook, was originally buried in the garden of his Sussex home but his remains were transferred to their present resting place in 1955.

Furzey Gardens, on the outskirts of the village, contains a beautiful selection of flowering plants laid out in the grounds of a 16th century cottage. They are open to visitors every day with the exception of Christmas Day and Boxing Day and are well worth a visit.

Minstead's public house is called The Trusty Servant after the famous picture belonging to Winchester College. The inn sign is a reproduction of this picture and a poem explaining the attributes of the strange creature it portrays is displayed on the front of the verandah.

From Cadnam take the A31 towards Ringwood and after 1 mile turn left at the top of the hill on to the road signposted 'Minstead ¾'. Follow this road for ½ mile passing two turnings to the left and one to the right. Just beyond a thatched cottage on the right called 'Yew Tree', park on the wide grass verge on the left opposite a stile on the right.

Start the walk by going on along the road to where there is a cottage on the right and bear slightly left to take a footpath that runs parallel to the road. Where this path rejoins the road carry straight on, passing a T-junction on your right and another turning to the left. Just beyond this turn right on to a lane marked

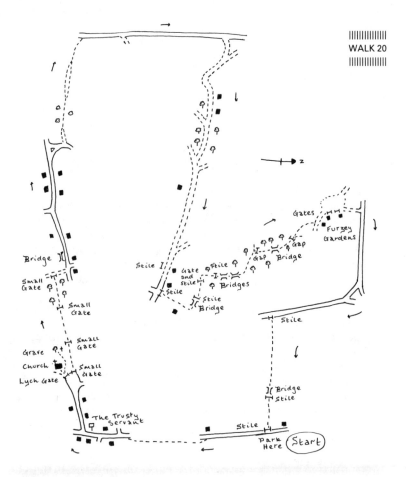

'Footpath to church'. The lane leads past The Trusty Servant inn on the right and just beyond it a pair of cottages which were once a technical school started by the lord of the manor.

The lane ends at the church. To find Sir Arthur Conan Doyle's grave go through the lych gate and take the right-hand path. Pass to the right of the church tower and follow a narrow grassy path to an oak tree at the rear of the churchyard. The grave is to the right of the tree.

To continue the walk go back through the lych gate and turn left. At the corner of the churchyard turn left again and follow a narrow path that leads straight ahead through two small gates to skirt a field beyond the graveyard. At the far side of the field the path goes through another gate into a wood and then eventually emerges through a fourth gate on to a track.

Turn right and then left on to the road. Cross a narrow bridge beside the ford and go on up the hill. Pass a road junction on the left and carry straight on until you reach another junction on the right. Turn right here and then, as the lane swings right, left on to a gravel track marked 'Bridleway'. Within a few yards this becomes a path leading through bushes and then widens to a track once more before narrowing again as it approaches the road.

Turn right to follow the verge, passing one track on the right. When you reach a second, turn right. The track is joined by another from the left as it swings right and then left to enter the trees. Ignore a track to the right and carry straight on. The track merges with one from the right, is joined by another from the left and then descends a slope. At the bottom there is another track to the left but still go straight ahead passing a stile in the hedge to the right.

Where the tarmac begins and there is a lane to the right, turn left to cross a stile on to a narrow path that runs between a fence on the right and a hedge on the left. After some distance the path swings left to cross a small plank bridge with a stile on the far side and then climbs a slight slope to a gate and stile.

Just beyond this stile turn right to follow a path down through the trees. It leads to another stile and two small bridges, the second of which is made out of logs. After this the path winds up a slope with a fence on the right.

Near the top turn right through a gap in the fence and follow the path to a plank bridge. On the far side it climbs a slope, passes through another gap in a fence and divides. Keep to the left fork. It goes straight ahead and joins a track. Turn left to follow the track for a short distance to where it emerges on to an expanse of open ground that is used as Furzey Gardens car park. Carry straight on, passing the entrance to the gardens on your right, to reach another track that leads down to a lane. Turn right and walk along the lane to the first turning on the right and then turn right and right again.

After a few hundred yards there is a stile on the left. Cross it and follow the hedge on the left to the far corner of the field where there is a plank bridge and another stile. Continue to go straight ahead along the edge of the next field and you will reach the stile that gives access to the road where you parked your car.

HOLIDAYS HILL INCLOSURE

WALK 21

★

3½ miles (5.5 km)

OS Landranger 195

Holidays Hill Inclosure lies to the south-west of Lyndhurst in an area that contains some of the most interesting features to be found in the New Forest. Not far from the car park is a Portuguese fireplace. This is a relic of the First World War when Portuguese troops were stationed here to help the depleted local labour force produce timber for the war effort. The fireplace, once part of the cookhouse, is retained as a memorial and was restored by the Forestry Commission with financial assistance from the Portuguese government.

In the middle of Holidays Hill Inclosure there is a grove of newly planted hardwoods. These young trees were provided by the members of the south of England Rotary Clubs to replace a stand of conifers that fell during the terrific gales of 1990 when damage was sustained throughout the area. The grove, which is known as Rotary Wood, was initially the idea of the New Milton Rotary Club. It consists of 1,728 oak seedlings and three slightly larger oak trees which are planted beside the track.

The Monarch's Grove is a small inclosure containing 18 small oak trees. These were planted in 1979 to mark the ninth centenary of the founding of the forest by William the Conqueror. Each of the little trees represents a reigning monarch who visited the forest during its long history.

In the centre of the Monarch's Grove stands the Knightwood Oak. This is one of the largest trees in the New Forest. It is over 300 years old and has been pollarded. This is an old custom no longer practised in the forest. When a tree was pollarded the top section of the trunk was removed so that the branches grew fairly close to the ground and the foliage was within reach of the forest animals.

Not far from the Knightwood Oak is Holidays Hill Cottage where there is a collection of amphibians and reptiles. Nearly every species of these creatures to be found in the British Isles is represented here.

Because this walk goes through the collection it is not one on which you can take your dog. For safety reasons pets are not allowed in the grounds of Holidays Hill Cottage.

Leave the A35 just west of Lyndhurst to take the road signposted 'Emery Down ¼'. Turn left at the New Forest Inn on to the road marked 'Bolderwood 4 — Linwood 7' and follow it for just over a mile. At this point Millyford Bridge car park is on the right.

Walk back to the road, cross over and turn right to follow the verge. This will lead you past a barbecue site on the left and, just beyond it, the Portuguese fireplace.

Carry on along the verge for a short distance and then turn left through a gate into the inclosure. Follow the gravel track straight ahead and where it divides take the right-hand fork. Walk along this for about 25 yards and then turn right again on to another gravel track that almost immediately curves to the left. Keep to this track ignoring a grassy one to the left, another to the right and a third which crosses it.

WALK 21

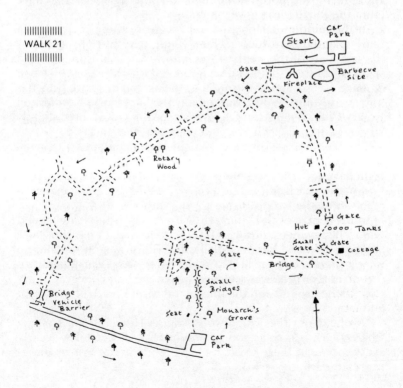

After this the track swings left again. It is joined by another grassy track on the right and just beyond it Rotary Wood will be seen on the left. Then there is another grassy track to the right and one to the left as the main track swings left yet again.

The track descends a slight slope and near the bottom it is crossed by yet another track. Disregard it and keep to the main track as it curves to the right. Ignore two tracks to the right and when you come to a grassy cross track, turn right. Follow this track through the trees ignoring all side turnings until, having crossed a low bridge, it emerges on to the road. Turn left and walk along the road until you come to Knightwood Oak car park on the left.

Go into the car park and turn left on to a narrow path signposted 'To Knightwood Oak'. This path will bring you to a small fenced inclosure. This is the Monarch's Grove and the Knightwood Oak is in the centre.

At the Monarch's Grove the path divides. Take the left-hand branch, passing the grove on your right, and follow the path to where it turns right beside the inclosure fence. Leave it at this point and turn left along the bank keeping the fence on your right. After about 100 yards the path swings left away from the fence. Follow it to where it joins a grassy track and turn right. Ignore a path that crosses the track and carry straight on.

This will eventually bring you to where the track joins a gravel one. Follow the gravel track straight ahead for a very short distance and then turn right on to a grassy track. This leads to a gate. Go through it and follow the path straight ahead. This will bring you to a bridge over a stream. Cross it and head up the slope towards a white building. This is Holidays Hill Cottage. Turn left just before it to go through a small gate between a Forestry Commission sign and another marked 'Car park'. Walk straight ahead to pass a hut on your left. The tanks containing the amphibians and reptiles are on your right.

Leave the cottage grounds by a track leading through a gate behind the tanks. Ignore a grassy track which crosses it and another that leads to the left and keep to the main track until you come to where it forks. Take the right-hand branch. It returns to the gate that opens on to the road. Turn right and follow the verge back to the car park on the left.

RHINEFIELD ORNAMENTAL DRIVE

WALK 22

★

2½ miles (4 km)

OS Landranger 195

This is one of the most attractive of the New Forest walks. It includes a large number of features to interest the naturalist and the easy walking conditions make it an ideal choice for a family outing. The walk is particularly lovely in early summer when the trees are in full leaf and the rhododendrons lining the ornamental drive are in flower.

The ornamental drive gets its name from Rhinefield Lodge, which was originally the home of the Master Keeper. Before the present road was built in 1938 the lodge was approached by a gravel drive. In 1859 an avenue of young conifers was planted along the length of this drive. It consists of a wide variety of species including redwood, Douglas fir, Austrian pine and deodar cedar. In the century since they were planted many of these trees have grown to be the tallest of their kind in the British Isles.

Vinney Ridge Inclosure is one of the oldest inclosures in the New Forest. It was first set aside for growing oak and beech in 1700. In those days large numbers of these hardwood trees were needed to build the wooden sailing ships on which Britain depended for her trade and defence. The young trees were protected by a ditch bordering a 6 ft high bank with a wooden fence on top to keep out deer, cattle and ponies.

Black Water is one of many streams draining this part of the forest. It is a tributary of the Lymington river and gains its name from the dark colour of its water. This becomes discoloured as it passes through the peat bogs further north.

Take the A35 from Lyndhurst travelling towards Bournemouth. After 2 miles turn left at the crossroads on to the narrow road signposted 'Rhinefield'. Within a very short distance the road becomes lined with laurel and rhododendron bushes. Pass a gravel track which crosses the road at right-angles and turn right just beyond it into Brock Hill car park.

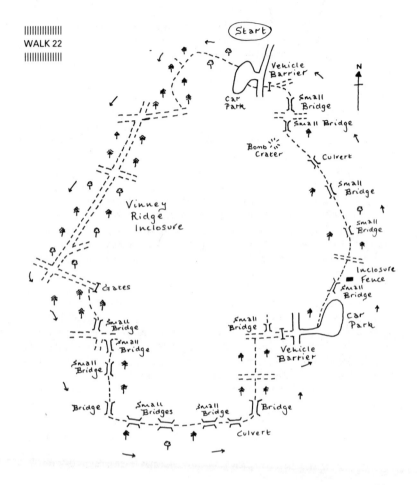

Leave the car park by the path in the rear right-hand corner. This is labelled 'Brock Hill Walk'. It leads up a slope through a grove of oak and beech trees and then swings left into a stand of young conifers. Ignore a path which heads down a steep slope to the right and continue along the main path until it turns left once more and is joined by a grassy track from the right. Turn right on to this and follow it for a short distance to where it is crossed by a gravel track, then turn left.

Where this track is crossed by another, carry straight on. You will soon come to an area where young fir trees are interspersed with older hardwoods. The track leads on through these trees until, having been joined by a grassy track from the left, it is crossed by another gravel one.

Turn left on to this track and follow it until you reach the place where it is barred by a pair of gates. Do not go through these gates but turn right beside them on to a gravel path which skirts the fence on the left for a short distance before winding away through the trees.

The path crosses a plank bridge, turns left to follow the course of a grassy track for a short distance and then, having passed another grassy track on the right, swings right to cross two more small bridges. It then leads on through the trees to a larger wooden bridge which spans the Black Water.

On the far side of this bridge turn sharp left to cross a small plank bridge and follow the gravel path along the bank. It crosses two more plank bridges and a culvert before swinging left once more to recross the Black Water by a second larger bridge.

Go over the bridge and continue along the path. It cuts across a grassy track and then meets a gravel one that leads to a gate on the left. Turn right on to this and, ignoring a path which crosses a bridge on the left, follow it past the vehicle barrier to the road. Cross over and turn left to skirt the car park and reach the beginning of 'Tall Trees Walk', then follow the narrow gravel path straight ahead.

Within a short distance this will lead you past a reconstruction of the old inclosure fence on the right. This is just one of several interesting features which border the path and are marked by Forestry Commission signs.

The path crosses a grassy ride and then two small plank bridges and a culvert to reach a place where there is a bomb crater on the left. This was made during the Second World War at a time when the Germans were dropping a number of incendiary and high explosive bombs on the forest. Their intention was to burn down the trees and thus deprive Britain of an important source of timber.

Beyond the bomb crater the path swings to the right. It passes over another two plank bridges, between which it is crossed by a grassy ride, and then turns left to join the road. Cross over and you will find Brock Hill car park on your right.

73

THE RUFUS STONE

WALK 23

★

3½ miles (5.5 km)

OS Landranger 195

William Rufus was the son of William the Conqueror and became king in 1087. Thirteen years later he was shot in the back with an arrow whilst out hunting in the New Forest. Nobody really knows whether his death was an act of murder or who was responsible for it. The blame was cast upon one of his fellow huntsmen, Walter Tyrrell, Lord of Poix, who was forced to flee for his life after the incident. Yet Tyrrell, an excellent marksman, proclaimed to his dying day that he had nothing to do with the King's death.

The Rufus Stone, which stands in the New Forest just south-west of Cadnam, is said to mark the spot where William Rufus died. The original stone was erected in 1745 by Lord Delaware when he was Master Keeper at Bolderwood Lodge. It was later covered by an iron casing to protect it from vandals.

The area around Stoney Cross is high land from which there are magnificent views to the east. During the Second World War this part of the forest was used as an aerodrome and sections of the old runways are still to be seen here.

King's Garn Gutter is one of the many streams that drain the forest area. It gained its strange name because it runs through what was once a garn or garden where the king's beehives were kept.

Take the A31 from Ringwood travelling towards Winchester and after 8 miles turn left on to the road marked 'Fritham 2 — Bolderwood 5 — Linwood 6'. Follow this road for ½ mile and turn right into Stoney Cross car park.

Walk back to the entrance of the car park and turn left on to the section of old runway that borders the road. Where this comes to an end continue along the verge until you come to the cattle grid. Just before it a track passes through a vehicle barrier on the left. Turn on to this track and follow it through the bushes, ignoring a path to the left that joins it near the vehicle barrier and then another to the right further on.

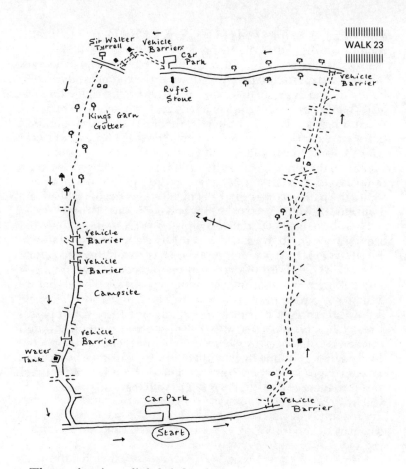

The track swings slightly left as it approaches the road and runs for a short distance beside a fence on the right before heading straight along the ridge, from which there are good views to the left. Ignore three small paths to the right and one to the left and where the track divides three ways take the centre branch. This goes straight ahead passing a clump of trees on the left. Within a few yards the track branches again. Take the right-hand fork. This will bring you to where the track narrows to a path and is crossed by two tracks from the right that converge on the left. Ignore them and carry straight on to follow the path through the bushes.

At the far side the path merges with a track from the right at a point where there is a narrow path on the left. Follow the track straight ahead. Ignore a path and another track which cross the track you are on, a path to the right and another cross path, and carry straight on until you reach the road. Turn left to follow the road down the hill to the Rufus Stone which is on the left.

Cross over to reach the Rufus Stone car park and take the track marked 'Access to cottage'. Walk down to the cottage and turn left beside the garden gate to follow the hedge on the right. This will lead you through two vehicle barriers and past another cottage to reach the road. Turn right to pass the Sir Walter Tyrrell public house on your right and cross the road near the far end of its car park. This will lead you past a 'Feeding of Animals Prohibited' sign on to the grass. Veer slightly right, passing between a clump of bushes on the left and a hedge on the right, to reach a point where the path becomes more distinct. It leads straight ahead and then dips down to a stream. This is King's Garn Gutter.

There is no bridge but it is usually easy to cross unless there has been heavy rain. In this case follow the bank for a short distance to the left where the stream narrows and it is possible to step across.

Follow the path up the slope on the far side of the stream. It emerges on to an expanse of grass and curves slightly left before climbing again to eventually join the end of a concrete track. Follow this straight ahead, ignoring any side turnings. It passes through a vehicle barrier into a campsite and then on through another two barriers to where the campsite ends. Beyond the third barrier continue to go straight ahead, passing a water tank on your right, and then continue along the track as it curves round to meet the road. Turn left to walk back to the car park, which is on the left.

WILVERLEY
AND THE NAKED MAN

WALK 24

★

5 miles (8 km)

OS Landranger 195

This walk provides a wide variety of scenery and interesting features. Parts of it cross open heathland, others lead through mature inclosures or traverse the wide expanses of grass known as lawns where the forest ponies and cattle graze. From Wilverley Plain there are magnificent views across the forest and near the beginning of the walk the tall column of Sway Tower can be seen on the horizon to the south.

Sway Tower, or Peterson's Folly as it is sometimes called, was built during the latter half of the 19th century by Judge Peterson in an effort to relieve local unemployment and to prove that concrete is a durable building material. When it was first erected the tower, which is 218 ft high, had a light on the top. However, this proved to be a great hazard to sailors in the Solent who mistook it for a lighthouse and so the Admiralty demanded that the light be removed.

The track leading across Wilverley Plain to the Naked Man is a section of an ancient ridgeway and was once part of a well-used route between Burley and Lymington. During the 18th and early 19th centuries, when smuggling was rife in the forest area, it was often used by smugglers on their nocturnal excursions to bring contraband inland.

The Naked Man, which stands to the right of this track near the point where it joins the main road, is the remains of an oak tree that has been struck by lightning. It was once used as a gibbet.

Leave the A35, Christchurch to Lyndhurst road, at Holmsley and follow signs to Brockenhurst and Setthorns. Where the road forks beyond the cattle grid take the left-hand branch, marked 'Brockenhurst and Lymington'. This will lead you up a slope, passing the entrance to a car park on the right. Not far beyond it a gravel track leads to a second car park at the edge of the inclosure on the left. This is Wilverley Inclosure car park.

Walk back along the gravel track to the road and turn right to

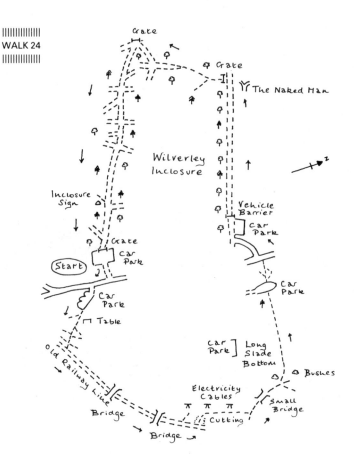

follow the verge to the car park sign. Cross over and take the gravel track, bearing right through Yew Tree Bottom car park. In the far left-hand corner of the car park a narrow path leads to a picnic place. Follow this for a short distance and then bear slightly left to walk down through the valley, passing a wooden picnic table on your left. Ignore two paths on the left, one on the right and a fourth that crosses the main path and carry straight on to reach an embankment which once supported a railway line to Brockenhurst. Climb the embankment and turn left to follow the course of the old railway.

Continue along the embankment until you have passed under two bridges. Beyond the second the banks become lower. Ignore a path that climbs the left-hand bank and then turn left through a narrow cutting which gives access to the lawn beyond. Some

78

electric cables supported on wooden posts cross the lawn at this point. Turn right and follow them to a gravel path that comes through a broken railway bridge on the right.

Turn left on to this path. It crosses a low concrete bridge over a stream and then divides three ways. Take the left-hand fork. This cuts through the gorse bushes to the lawn.

Head straight across the lawn, keeping to the valley. Ignore a car park on the hill to the left and carry on towards a second at the far side of the grass. This will take you through a place at the head of the valley where the lawn narrows. Keep to the right of a lone pine tree and cross the turning circle at the lower end of the car park to take a narrow path that climbs a slight slope straight ahead.

Keep to the main path, ignoring a branch to the right and another to the left, until you reach the road and then cross over on to a metalled track that gives access to Wilverley Plain car park and picnic area. At the T-junction turn right to walk through the car park and on along the track straight ahead, keeping the inclosure on your left. This track is the old smugglers' road and will eventually lead you past the Naked Man, which is enclosed by a wooden fence to protect it from the forest animals.

Having passed the Naked Man on the right, turn left through a gate into the inclosure. Follow the path straight ahead for a short distance to where it divides and then take the right-hand fork. This winds away through the trees and slowly widens into a track.

When you come to the place where this track is crossed by another, turn right and walk up to the gate that gives access to the road. Do not go through the gate: turn sharp left beside it on to a gravel track that leads away from the road.

Carry straight on ignoring all side turnings until you reach the place where the main gravel track divides. Keep to the left-hand branch. After a short distance it is crossed by a grassy ride and then leads down a slope through the trees. Disregard a secondary track to the right near the bottom of the hill and a cross track in the valley and follow the main track on up the next slope.

After some distance it is joined by a path from the right and then a track on the left. At this point there is an interesting old inclosure sign on the right. This was placed here during the last century and gives a short account of the history of Wilverley Inclosure.

Disregard the track to the left and carry straight on. This will lead you past a track that leads down a slope to the right, beyond which is a gate opening on to the car park.

EYEWORTH POND

WALK 25

★

7 miles (11 km)

OS Landranger 184 and 195

This walk is one of the best for those who wish to sample a variety of New Forest scenery. Parts of it run across open heathland whilst others lead through oak woods. Bramshaw Telegraph is one of the highest places in this part of the forest and Eyeworth Pond is one of the New Forest beauty spots. It is a very picturesque spot in early summer when the water is dotted with clumps of water lilies.

Leave the M27 at junction 1 and take the B3078 signposted 'Fordingbridge'. Having turned left opposite The Bell Inn in Brook village, continue to follow the road for just over 3 miles to where the B3078 and the B3080 diverge. Just before the junction turn left into Telegraph Hill car park.

Return to the road and turn left and left again onto a track that leads through a vehicle barrier. Ignore three paths to the left and a cross path and where the track divides take the left-hand fork. This goes through the edge of the wood and as it enters the trees it branches again. Still keep to the left fork which merges with first one and then another track from the right. Beyond these ignore a path and two tracks to the left and then a cross path.

Where the track forks take the right-hand branch. Ignore a rather overgrown track to the left and another cross path and carry straight on to reach a group of holly trees. Two tracks lead away to the left but disregard them and go straight ahead.

Pass another track to the left, one to the right and a third that crosses the track you are following. Beyond this there is a small brick building on the right. Ignore a track to the right and continue to where the main track meets another in a T-junction.

Turn left and follow the track down the slope. At the bottom it is joined by another coming through a gate to the right. Ignore it and carry straight on, disregarding two tracks to the right and two larger ones to the left as the main one winds through the wood.

After crossing a bridge over a small stream the track swings sharp left at a point where a grassy track leads straight ahead.

80

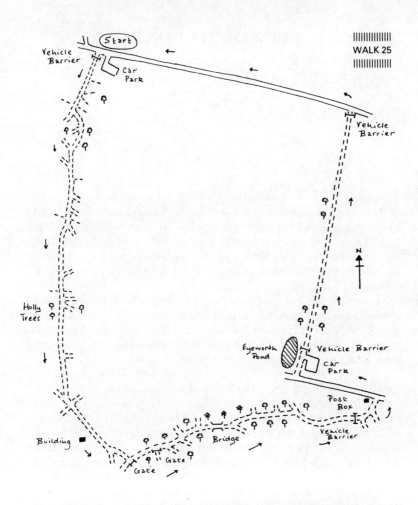

Ignore this grassy track and another three that join the gravel one on the left further along. Just after the third of these the track begins a long climb up a slope and eventually passes through a vehicle barrier, beyond which it is joined by another track from the right. Ignore this and carry straight on to follow the track round to the left where it meets a lane.

Turn left and walk down the lane to Eyeworth Pond. Where the tarmac ends turn right on to a track which leads to Eyeworth Pond car park, passing the pond on your left. Pass the car park on your right and take the track going straight ahead through a vehicle barrier. This will bring you to a road. Turn left to follow the verge back to Telegraph Hill where the car park is on the left.

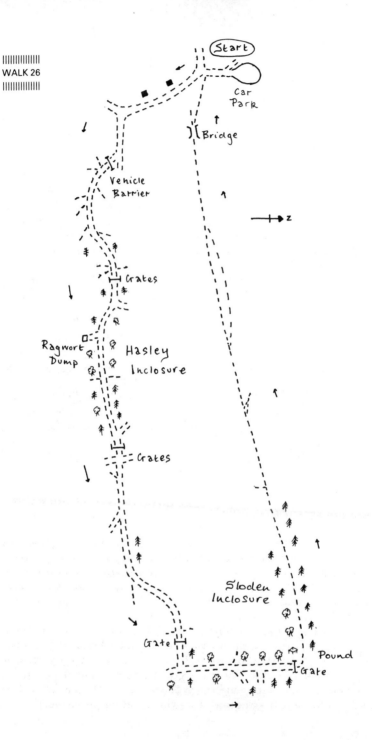

Start

Car Park

Bridge

Vehicle Barrier

Grates

Ragwort Dump

Hasley Inclosure

Grates

Sloden Inclosure

Gate

Pound

Gate

z

OGDENS

WALK 26

★

4 miles (6 km)

OS Landranger 195

Ogdens is situated in one of the most beautiful parts of the New Forest where softly rounded, heather-clad hills are interspersed with inclosures of mixed woodland and the little Latchmore brook meanders through a wide valley on its way to join the Avon. The expanse of grass in this valley is a favourite feeding ground for the forest animals and also provides some excellent picnic sites.

In Hasley Inclosure a small fenced area is used as a ragwort dump. Ragwort grows in many parts of the forest but its toxic properties make it a danger to livestock. During the summer months large quantities of it are uprooted and brought to this secluded place to rot.

On the grassy ride to the north of Sloden Inclosure there is a pound. This is used when the ponies are rounded up for branding. Its outer fence forms a sort of funnel into which the animals can be driven with ease.

Take the A338 from Ringwood travelling towards Salisbury and after 2¼ miles turn right on to a road signposted 'Mockbeggar ¾ — South Gorley 1¼'. Follow this road to the crossroads and turn left. This is signposted 'North Gorley 1½ — Stuckton 2¾'. Continue along this road for ¾ mile and turn right on to the lane to Furze Hill. This is the second turning on the right. After just over a mile the lane swings left towards Hyde at a point where the Fir Tree Equestrian Centre is on the right. Leave it at this point to take the 'No through road' straight ahead. Where this ends carry on along the track and then turn left into Ogdens car park.

Walk back to the car park entrance and turn left on to a track that skirts a fence on the right. Where the track swings left ignore a branch to the right labelled 'Cottage only — no parking' and carry on to reach a point where the track divides. Take the right-hand fork, which passes through a vehicle barrier and then swings left on to the open heathland. Keep to the track ignoring all side turnings until eventually you reach a pair of gates opening on to an inclosure. Go through the smaller gate and continue to follow the track straight ahead.

The track swings right and then divides. Take the right-hand fork. It veers slightly left to skirt a fence on the left that protects a plantation of young hardwoods. A short track to the right gives access to the ragwort dump and then within a short distance the track leaves the fence behind and continues through stands of more mature trees. It is crossed by a path but ignore this and carry straight on. The trees on the right slowly begin to thin, affording glimpses of the beautiful view across the valley and then the track is joined by another from the left as it approaches the gates at the far side of the inclosure.

Ignore a cross track on the far side of the gates and continue to follow the track straight ahead. Where it divides keep to the left-hand fork that goes straight on to pass a clump of fir trees on the left. Disregard a path leading up a slope as the track swings left and continue along the track to reach the gate at the edge of Sloden Inclosure.

Just before the gate there is a cross path but keep to the track, following it into the inclosure where it meets another track in a T-junction. Turn left and when the track divides at a point where there is a grassy path to the left, take the left-hand fork which leads straight ahead. Disregard a grassy track to the right and carry on until you reach a gate. Go through it and turn left to pass the pound on your left and follow the grassy ride between the inclosures.

Where the trees end take the path straight ahead, ignoring a turning to the left. The path runs through the valley. Ignore a narrow path that diverges from it to the right and where the main path divides take either fork for they both lead straight on and eventually rejoin.

Beyond this the path leads across a wide expanse of open grassland and eventually crosses a low concrete bridge over a ditch. On the far side it divides. Follow the branch to the right. It runs to the head of the track that leads back down to the car park on the right.

WOODGREEN

WALK 27

★

3 miles (4.5 km)

OS Landranger 184

The village of Woodgreen lies on the north-western edge of the New Forest at a point where the river Avon forms the forest boundary. It is bordered to the east by pleasant inclosures of mature soft and hardwood trees beyond which there are fine views across the open heathland towards Godshill.

To the south of the village is Castle Hill, thought to be the site of the only Norman fortification in the forest area. The hill slopes steeply down to the river and from the crest there is a magnificent view across the valley towards Fordingbridge and Breamore.

Take the A338 from Ringwood travelling towards Salisbury and turn right in Breamore on to the road signposted 'Woodgreen 1 — Hale 3'. Having crossed the cattle grid at the beginning of Woodgreen village, take the first turning on the right passing the post office on your right. This is the road to Godshill. Follow it for about a mile to where, having left the village behind, it swings sharp left and is joined by a gravel lane on the right. Just beyond this point turn right into Godshill car park.

Walk back to the car park entrance and turn left to follow the edge of the road. Leave it where it swings right and go along the gravel lane keeping the inclosure fence on your right. Within a short distance the gravel lane meets a metalled one that comes up a slope on the left. Just past this point there is a pair of gates in the inclosure fence on the right.

Go through the smaller gate beyond which three paths diverge. Take the central one. It runs straight ahead through the trees and joins a gravel track. Cross this and take the grassy track straight ahead. Ignore a turning to the left and, where the track divides, take the right-hand branch. This leads straight ahead and quickly degenerates into a path, which again divides. This time keep to the left-hand branch. It leads straight on through the trees and eventually swings slightly left to end at a pair of gates opening on to the road at Castle Hill. Directly opposite and to the left are viewpoints overlooking the wide expanse of the Avon valley.

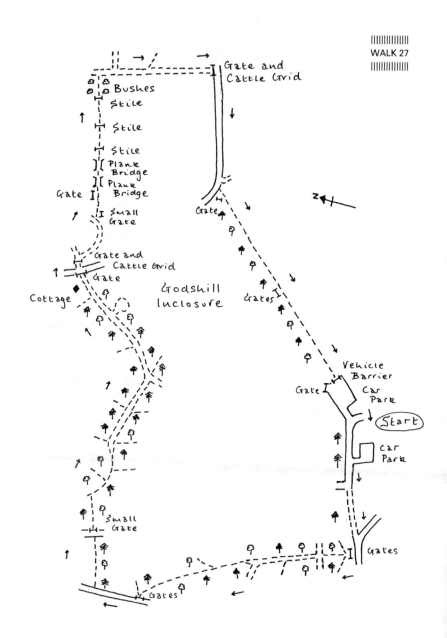

Gate and Cattle Grid

Bushes
Stile
Stile
Stile
Plank Bridge
Plank Bridge
Gate
Small Gate
Gate

Gate and Cattle Grid
Gate
Cottage

Godshill Inclosure

Gate

Gates

Vehicle Barrier
Car Park
Gate
Start

Car Park

Small Gate

Gates
Gates

Having left the inclosure turn right to follow the verge. Within about 100 yards the fence on the right comes to an end. Turn right at this point to take a narrow path which leads down a bank, keeping the inclosure fence on your right. This will soon bring you to another road. Cross it and go through a small gate on the far side, then follow the path straight ahead. It winds through the trees to join a second path. Bear right on to this.

Ignore one path to the left and another to the right beyond which the main path begins to widen into a track. It is crossed by two more paths and eventually joins a gravel track in a T-junction at a point where a grassy path leads straight ahead. Turn left on to the gravel track and follow it, ignoring all side turnings, to where, having passed a cottage on the left, it ends at a gate that opens on to the road.

Cross over to take a track directly opposite the gate. It is labelled 'Footpath' and curves to the right over a cattle grid with a small gate beside it. On the far side of the cattle grid it divides. Keep to the right-hand fork and, where the track swings left to end at a house, take the path straight ahead, passing a small wooden gate on your right. The path skirts a large wooden gate on the left, crosses two small plank bridges and leads up a slope to a stile. Cross this and the field beyond to reach another stile in the fence on the far side. This gives access to a second field. Walk straight across it to a stile in the hedge from which a narrow path leads down to a track.

Turn right to follow the track, ignoring another marked 'Bridleway' that leads away to the left. When you come to the road turn right and walk along the edge to where it swings sharp right towards Woodgreen. At this point go straight ahead across the grass keeping the inclosure fence on your right.

Ignore a pair of gates leading into the inclosure and continue to follow the fence until eventually you come to a car park. There are good views from here across the open heathland to the left.

Walk straight across the car park to the road and then bear right to follow the verge. This will bring you back to Godshill car park on the left.

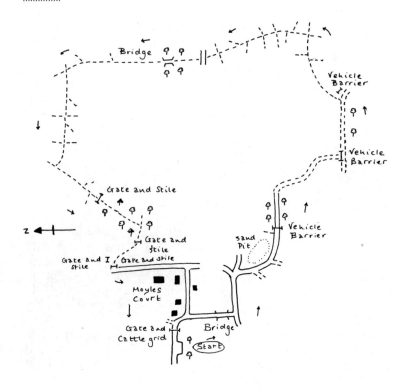

FINE, WET UNDERFOOT
BLAND.

MOYLES COURT

WALK 28

★

4 miles (6 km)

OS Landranger 195

Moyles Court is a large 16th century house at Ellingham on the western edge of the New Forest. It was once the home of Dame Alice Lisle, who was sentenced to death by Judge Jeffreys for giving shelter to two fugitives during the Monmouth Rebellion, and is now a private school.

The part of the forest to the east of Moyles Court is very beautiful. Its high, heather-clad hills afford magnificent views towards Salisbury in the north and across the Avon valley to the west.

Many parts of this area of the Avon valley have been used for the extraction of sand and gravel. In some places the pits resulting from this activity have later been flooded and given a new lease of life as venues for sporting activities.

Take the A338 from Ringwood travelling towards Salisbury and after 1½ miles turn right on to the road signposted 'Moyles Court ¾ — Linwood 2½'. Drive along this road for ¾ mile and park by the trees on the right just before the cattle grid sign on the left.

Walk on along the road and at the far side of the cattle grid turn right on to the road marked 'Rockford ½ — Poulner 1½ — Linwood 1¾'. It crosses a bridge and meets another road in a T-junction. Turn left following the sign 'Linwood 1¾'.

This will bring you to another junction. Turn right and then sharp right again. Ignore two tracks leading to some cottages on the right and follow the lane as it curves left up the hill, passing a sand pit on the left.

Beyond this the lane passes through a vehicle barrier and narrows to a track. Ignore a path to the left just before the barrier and keep to the track. It leads up a slope between tree-clad banks to emerge on to an expanse of grass at the top of the hill. Here the track becomes unmetalled as it winds its way across the hilltop and eventually joins another track in a T-junction.

Turn left to follow the track up a slight slope from which there are good views to the left. At the top the track is joined by a path that passes through a gap beside a vehicle barrier on the left. Turn left on to this. It runs along a ridge and then is joined by a path to the right and another to the left. Disregard both of these and carry straight on for a short distance to reach a cross path. Turn left here and follow the path round to the left, ignoring a narrow path to the right.

The path leads across the brow of the hill, from which there are magnificent views, and then begins to dip down towards the valley. Ignore a narrow path to the left at the top of the hill, two cross paths as it descends the slope and then another path to the left. Where the main path forks take the left-hand branch. This runs straight down the slope and crosses one more path to reach the road.

Go over the road and take the path straight ahead. It leads down a slight slope to a bridge over a stream and then begins the climb to the next ridge. From here it runs for some distance across the hilltop. Keep to the main path, ignoring a minor path to the right, and where it divides take the left fork. This almost immediately crosses another path. Turn left on to this and follow it straight ahead ignoring all side turnings until eventually it narrows and joins another wider path. Turn left to follow this towards a gate opening on to a wood. Just before the gate one of the flooded gravel pits can be seen in the valley to the right.

Cross the stile beside the gate and follow the path through the trees. It descends a slope to join another path from the left. Turn right and after a fairly short distance you will come to another gate with a stile beside it at the far side of the wood. Bear right across the field beyond to reach two gates and stiles in the corner of the field. Take the left-hand one which gives access to the road and turn left to follow the verge. This will lead you past Moyles Court on the right. At the far end of its grounds turn right on to a road signposted 'Ellingham 1 — Ringwood 3'. This will bring you to a junction. Bear right and then left over the cattle grid to reach your car.

BREAMORE
AND THE MIZMAZE

WALK 29

★

3½ miles (5.5 km)

OS Landranger 184

This is a pleasant walk through rolling downland countryside and includes several features of historical interest. Parts of the route run through the Breamore Estate and, although dogs are allowed in the area, they must be kept on leads during the latter half of the walk which passes the mizmaze and then runs through the woods behind Breamore House.

The mizmaze is one of the most fascinating historical sites in Hampshire. There are only seven such mazes left in the whole of England and this is the best preserved. It is over 30 yds in diameter and consists of a narrow grassy causeway that weaves its way between grooves of chalk to a central mound. Nobody knows its true age or original purpose but it is generally believed that it was used in some kind of religious rite by our pagan ancestors.

Breamore House is an imposing Tudor building which was skilfully restored after a fire in 1853. It was the home of the Hulse family for over 200 years and still contains a fine collection of paintings and furniture. During the summer months the house is often open to the public and there are two museums in the grounds. One is dedicated to agriculture and the other displays an interesting collection of carriages.

Close to the house is the church. It is the oldest in this part of Hampshire and the best example of a Saxon church in the county. Above the south door there is a badly damaged Saxon rood surmounted by the hand of God emerging from a cloud. The rood was deliberately mutilated at the time of the Reformation when the carving was cut back level with the wall. Another Saxon relic which luckily escaped this kind of attention is a sentence carved into one of the four arches supporting the tower. It is one of the few Saxon inscriptions to be found in England and means 'Here the Covenant becomes manifest to thee'.

Turn off the A338 in Breamore village on to the lane signposted 'Whitsbury 3½'. Where the lane forks take the left-hand branch and follow it to the T-junction. Park on the grass

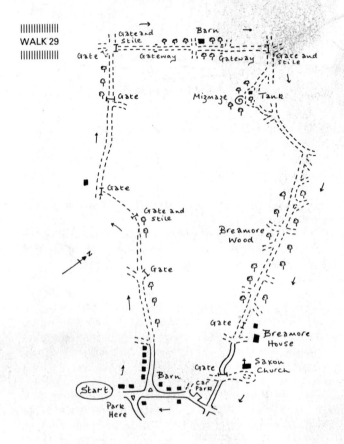

verge on the left just before the two roads meet.

Start the walk by turning right on to the road signposted to Breamore House and the Saxon church and then turn almost immediately left on to a lane which passes a barn on the right. Follow the lane to where it ends and then take the track straight ahead, ignoring a field entrance to the left marked 'Footpath'. The track leads up a slight slope, bears left and then forks at a point where there is a field entrance on the right. Take the right-hand fork which leads straight ahead.

The track soon narrows to a path that descends a slope to a gate with a stile set in the fence beside it. Cross the stile and follow the hedge on the left to reach another gate in the corner of the field. This gate opens on to a track. Turn right and walk along the track. It will take you past a farm on the left and then another in the valley to the right.

Not far beyond this the track forks. Keep to the left-hand branch. It leads straight ahead through a gate and is marked 'Bridleway only'. Follow it to where the trees on the left give way to a short expanse of grass and a track descends a slope to the left. Turn right at this point to cross a stile beside a field gate and follow the track towards a wood.

The track passes through a gateway at the corner of the wood and then skirts the trees to reach a place where two tracks cross. Carry straight on to pass a Dutch barn on your left and follow the track through the trees. At the far side it divides. Take the right-hand branch which is grass covered and leads up the slope with a fence on the right. This will bring you to a gate and stile giving access to a track at a point where a second track leads straight ahead.

Cross the stile and turn right to follow the track to where the fence on the right ends and the track forks. Take the right-hand branch leading up the slope towards the trees. At the top a narrow, rather indistinct, path goes into the wood. Turn right on to this, passing a metal tank on your left, and then head straight through trees to a fenced clearing containing the mizmaze.

Turn left to skirt the fence and leave it by a path to the left about a quarter of the way round. The path emerges from the wood and divides. Take the right-hand fork which runs down to join a track from the left. Turn right on to this and follow it as it curves to the left down the slope.

At the bottom it is joined by a track from the right and another from the left. Ignore these and carry straight on. The track is now bordered by trees and after some distance it forks. Keep to the right-hand branch. This almost immediately forks again but still keep to the right and follow the track into the trees.

From here the track goes down through the wood to the valley. Follow it straight ahead ignoring all side turnings. This will lead you past Breamore House on the left at the bottom of the hill. Disregard a track to the right opposite the house and carry on along the metalled drive to the gateway. Just beyond this a gravel track to the left leads to the Saxon church.

To continue the walk take the metalled lane straight ahead. Where this is crossed by another turn right, following the sign to Whitsbury. This will lead you past the entrance to Breamore House car park on the right, beyond which the lane curves left at a point where it is joined by a track from Home Farm on the right. Keep to the lane. After some distance it passes a turning on the right and then comes to the junction on the left where you parked your car.

MARTIN DOWN

★

3 miles (4.5 km)

OS Landranger 184

The open expanse of grassland known as Martin Down has not been part of Hampshire for very long. It came into the county during the late 19th century when the border between Hampshire and Wiltshire was altered slightly. In character it is much more like part of Wiltshire, being very similar to the neighbouring Salisbury Plain.

Today Martin Down is a National Nature Reserve which means that any dogs walked here must be kept under strict control. There is a great variety of wildlife on the down including the timid roe deer, the smallest species of deer native to the British Isles. They are just over 2 ft tall and their antlers are only 8 or 9 inches in length.

Martin Down also has several interesting historical features. One of these is Bokerley Ditch which runs along the western edge of the down marking the border between Hampshire and Dorset. This ditch and its attendant bank were built during Roman times to protect the area to the west of Martin Down from invasion.

To the east of Bokerley Ditch lies Grim's Ditch, another ancient earthwork consisting of two banks with a ditch between them. Much older than Bokerley Ditch, it is thought to date from the Middle Bronze Age.

Turn off the A354 on to the road signposted 'Martin 1½ — Damerham 4½ — Fordingbridge 8'. Drive into Martin village and take the second turning on the right. This is Sillens Lane. It has two entrances divided by a triangle of grass on which is situated an old pump. Follow the lane to its end and park on the grass straight ahead.

Leave the car park by the right-hand track which skirts the hedge. Ignore a set of three tracks on the left and where the main track divides keep to the left-hand fork. This is wider than the right-hand one and runs parallel to it.

After a short distance a path splits away from the track to the left and then runs beside it down a slope to reach a place where six

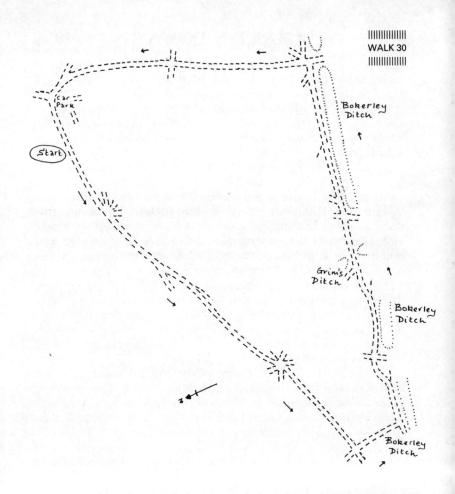

tracks meet. Take the track straight ahead, passing two tracks on
the left and two on the right. It runs up a slope from which there
are lovely views to the right, and is crossed by another track at the
top. Turn left onto this and follow it towards a gap in the high
bank on the horizon. This bank and the ditch beside it form the
earthwork known as Bokerley Ditch which, at this point, marks
the border between Hampshire and Dorset.

As it approaches Bokerley Ditch the track meets another in a
T-junction. Turn left onto this. It runs along beside the ditch for
some distance and then swings slightly left as a path diverges from
it to the right. Still keep to the track. It descends a slope, crosses
another track and then skirts the ditch once more before climbing
a slight incline to reach a place where it is joined by another track

95

from the left. Ignore this track and carry straight on to pass through a gap in a low earthwork. This is Grim's Ditch. The track then leads down into a valley where it is crossed by another track but ignore this and continue up the next slope, disregarding a track to the left near the bottom of the incline.

Ignore a path and then a track to the left and continue to where the track you are following meets a gravel one which cuts through the earthwork to the right. From this point there is a magnificent view across the valley to the left where Martin village nestles between Martin Down and Toyd Down. It is also a very good vantage point from which to spot the deer and other wild creatures that frequent the downs.

Turn left to follow the gravel track down the hill. Ignore a cross track near the bottom and go straight on to reach a place where two tracks merge. Bear left and within a very short distance you will be back at the place where you left the car.